AN AGE OF EMPIRES, 1₂
FILMS AND DOCUMENₜₐ₌ᵢₑₛ

Consider using the following films to stimulate student interest or for extension and enrichment. Teachers should preview all films and be aware that like historical fiction, films are not always accurate in details.

China's Forbidden City. Video from the History Channel's "In Search of History" series. For 500 years, the enormous palace complex known as the Forbidden City was the home of China's emperors and strictly off-limits for anyone but the royal attendants and family.

Christopher Columbus: Explorer of the New World. Video from A&E Biography. From the dream that led him across the horizon to the fortunes that deserted him and the ongoing controversy over his true place in history, this is the dramatic story of Christopher Columbus.

Genghis Khan–Terror and Conquest (1995). From A&E Biography. This documentary produced for television is about the military conquests of Genghis Khan and the Mongols.

Galileo's Battle for the Heavens. From PBS; originally aired October 2002.

The Inquisition (1999). History Channel video in the "History's Mysteries" series is also available on DVD. Reveals the myths and misconceptions that surround one of the darkest periods in the history of man and religion. Sometimes shocking, this movie should be reviewed especially carefully before showing to students.

Ivan the Terrible: Might and Madness (2000). An A&E Biography from the *Russia: Land of the Tsars* set. Available on DVD and VHS, this documentary produced for television discusses the life of Ivan the Terrible.

Splendors of the Ottoman Sultans (1992). This educational documentary explores the glory and might of the Ottoman Empire, and includes footage of over 270 objects—many of which have never been outside the borders of Turkey and the walls of Topkapi Palace.

Treasure! The Habsburg Family Jewels. From A&E Home Video. Helpful as a tool that illustrates the immense wealth of the Habsburgs. (While they ruled, the Habsburgs aggressively acquired the works of Europe's best artists.)

An Age of Empires
1200-1750

Teaching Guide

Oxford University Press, Inc., publishes works that
further Oxford University's objective of excellence
in research, scholarship, and education.

Oxford   New York
Auckland   Cape Town   Dar es Salaam   Hong Kong   Karachi
Kuala Lumpur   Madrid   Melbourne   Mexico City   Nairobi
New Delhi   Shanghai   Taipei   Toronto

With offices in
Argentina   Austria   Brazil   Chile   Czech Republic   France   Greece
Guatemala   Hungary   Italy   Japan   Poland   Portugal   Singapore
South Korea   Switzerland   Thailand   Turkey   Ukraine   Vietnam

Published by Oxford University Press, Inc.
198 Madison Avenue, New York, NY, 10016
www.oup.com

Oxford is a registered trademark of Oxford University Press

ISBN-13: 978-0-19-522257-9 (California edition)   ISBN-13: 978-0-19522348-4

Project Director: Jacqueline A. Ball
Education Consultant: Diane L Brooks, Ed.D.
Editors: Georgia Scurletis, Katherine Schulten
Design: dlabnyc

Casper Grathwohl, Publisher

Printed in the United States of America

CONTENTS

Note to the Teacher   5

The Medieval & Early Modern World Program   6
   Using the Teaching Guide and Student Study Guide

Improving Literacy with *The Medieval & Early Modern World*   16

Group Projects   20

Teaching Strategies for *An Age of Empires, 1200–1750*
   Chapter 1   Golden Khan, Golden Reins, Golden Horde: 26
                The Mongols Ride Out
   Chapter 2   Who's Next?: The Mongols Reach Their Limit   32
   Chapter 3   Twice As Powerful: Poland and Lithuania Unite   38
   Chapter 4   Troubled Times, Troubled Tsars: The Russian Empire   44
   Chapter 5   The Real Mughals, Not the Reel Moguls: Empire in India   50
   Chapter 6   Triumph of the Turks: The Rise of the Ottoman Empire   56
   Chapter 7   When Tents Become Towers: The Sultans Settle Down   62
   Chapter 8   Stocking the Royal Spice Cabinet: The Portuguese Empire   68
   Chapter 9   "Go Further!": Spain Expands Across an Ocean   74
   Chapter 10   The Wedding Ring Empire: Europe under the Habsburgs   80
   Chapter 11   Teenagers Take the Throne: Manchu China   86

Wrap-Up Test   92

Rubrics   94

Graphic Organizers   98

Answer Key (Teaching Guide and Student Study Guide)   106

HISTORY FROM OXFORD UNIVERSITY PRESS

"A thoroughly researched political and cultural history... makes for a solid resource for any collection."
– *School Library Journal*

THE WORLD IN ANCIENT TIMES
RONALD MELLOR AND AMANDA H. PODANY, EDS.
THE EARLY HUMAN WORLD
THE ANCIENT NEAR EASTERN WORLD
THE ANCIENT EGYPTIAN WORLD
THE ANCIENT SOUTH ASIAN WORLD
THE ANCIENT CHINESE WORLD
THE ANCIENT GREEK WORLD
THE ANCIENT ROMAN WORLD
THE ANCIENT AMERICAN WORLD

"Bringing history out of the Dark Ages!"

THE MEDIEVAL AND EARLY MODERN WORLD
BONNIE G. SMITH, ED.
THE EUROPEAN WORLD, 400–1450
THE AFRICAN AND MIDDLE EASTERN WORLD, 600–1500
THE ASIAN WORLD, 600–1500
AN AGE OF EMPIRES, 1200–1750
AN AGE OF VOYAGES, 1350–1600
AN AGE OF SCIENCE AND REVOLUTIONS, 1600–1800

"The liveliest, most realistic, most well-received American history series ever written for children."
– *Los Angeles Times*

A HISTORY OF US
JOY HAKIM
THE FIRST AMERICANS
MAKING THIRTEEEN COLONIES
FROM COLONIES TO COUNTRY
THE NEW NATION
LIBERTY FOR ALL?
WAR, TERRIBLE WAR
RECONSTRUCTING AMERICA
AN AGE OF EXTREMES
WAR, PEACE, AND ALL THAT JAZZ
ALL THE PEOPLE

FOR MORE INFORMATION, VISIT US AT WWW.OUP.COM

New from Oxford University Press
Reading History, by Janet Allen
ISBN 0-19-516595-0 hc 0-19-516596-9 pb

"*Reading History* is a great idea. I highly recommend this book."
–Dennis Denenberg, *Professor of Elementary and Early Childhood Education, Millersville University*

Strategic Methods for Content Learning
READING HISTORY
A PRACTICAL GUIDE TO IMPROVING LITERACY

JANET ALLEN
with Christine Landaker

NOTE TO THE TEACHER

Dear Fellow Educator:

How do we realize our hopes and dreams? How do we face the challenges of everyday life? Everyone—old and young alike—asks such questions at one time or another. One place to look for answers is in the lives of people in the past. In history we find ordinary people building cathedrals and mosques, conducting trade over thousands of miles, eking out a living through agriculture and crafts, and dreaming dreams of creating vast empires. This series brings you their stories.

As educators, we want to present these stories as part of a living past—and the authors of our books aim to provide you with the materials to do just that. We offer ways to make the past come alive with vivid images in full color, lively accounts of actual people, and maps to show young readers where these people lived and how they traveled the world. Heroes tell us in their own words of their noblest hopes; villains show us their cruelty. Ordinary folks face the plague and young boys set out in creaky ships on dangerous seas. This series helps you show young adults the fullness of the past and the grand achievements that make up our heritage.

We all know that our task does not stop at presenting the *story* of the past. We must also teach our students the *skills* vital to understanding history and to becoming informed citizens. These books are designed to help you train students to think critically about human opinions, prejudices, and programs for the future. The many voices from historical actors in the series provide opportunities for students to come to terms with burning issues of bias and point of view.

You and I share not only great hopes for the future but also the daily challenges of teaching. In addition to the stories, images, quotes, maps, timelines, and young adult bibliographies of the books themselves, the series includes instructional guides with tested ideas for teaching the medieval and early modern world. These guides are filled with exercises, classroom activities, and daily lessons based on specific chapters in each book. They show additional, practical ways to make critical thinking an integral part of your work in world history.

The authors of the student books and the supporting instructional materials bring you and your students the very latest thinking about what world history is. We urge you to tell us how their presentation of this vital, emerging field works with your students. Good history, like the creation of civilization itself, depends on our common effort!

Bonnie G. Smith
General Editor

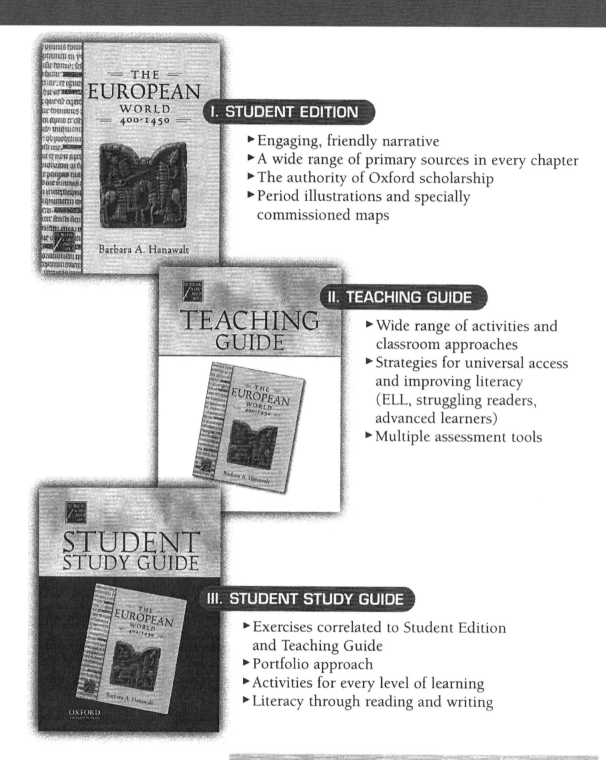

I. STUDENT EDITION

- ▸ Engaging, friendly narrative
- ▸ A wide range of primary sources in every chapter
- ▸ The authority of Oxford scholarship
- ▸ Period illustrations and specially commissioned maps

II. TEACHING GUIDE

- ▸ Wide range of activities and classroom approaches
- ▸ Strategies for universal access and improving literacy (ELL, struggling readers, advanced learners)
- ▸ Multiple assessment tools

III. STUDENT STUDY GUIDE

- ▸ Exercises correlated to Student Edition and Teaching Guide
- ▸ Portfolio approach
- ▸ Activities for every level of learning
- ▸ Literacy through reading and writing

PRIMARY SOURCES AND REFERENCE VOLUME

- ▸ Broad selection of primary sources in each subject area
- ▸ Ideal resource for in-class exercises and unit projects

The Teaching Guides organize each *Medieval & Early Modern World* book into chapter-based lessons of six (6) pages each, preceded by a special section that includes one longer-term project per chapter. These projects are cross-curricular, designed for mixed-group participation, and suitable for a wide range of learning styles. They can be used for teacher and student self- or peer assessment with the rubrics at the back of this Teaching Guide.

GROUP PROJECTS

Engaging, creative projects for group work on a wide variety of inviting topics

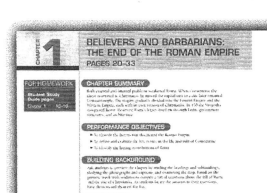

CHAPTER LESSONS

Teaching strategies and suggestions that address curriculum and that link with Student Study Guide and Student Edition

TESTS AND BLACKLINE MASTERS (BLMS)

Reproducible tests; map skills, primary sources, and document-based questions (DBQs) for assessment, homework, or classroom projects

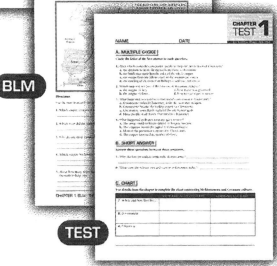

Teaching guides are organized so that you can easily find the information you need.

CHAPTER SUMMARY AND PERFORMANCE OBJECTIVES

The Chapter Summary gives an overview of the information in the chapter. The Performance Objectives are the three or four important goals students should achieve in the chapter. Accomplishing these goals will help students master the information in the book as well as meet standards for the course.

BUILDING BACKGROUND

This section connects students to the chapter they are about to read. Students may be asked to use what they know to make predictions about the text, preview the images in the chapter, or connect modern life with the historical subject matter.

VOCABULARY

A word list for every chapter defines difficult words and key curricular terms and recaps glossary entries.

CHAPTER 1

BELIEVERS AND BARBARIANS: THE END OF THE ROMAN EMPIRE
PAGES 20–33

FOR HOMEWORK

Student Study Guide pages
Chapter 1   13–16

CHAPTER SUMMARY

Both external and internal problems weakened Rome. When Constantine the Great converted to Christianity he moved the capital east to a city later renamed Constantinople. The empire gradually divided into the Eastern Empire and the Western Empire, each with its own version of Christianity. In 410 the Visigoths conquered Rome. However, Rome's legacy lived on through Latin, government structures, and architecture.

PERFORMANCE OBJECTIVES

- To identify the factors that threatened the Roman Empire
- To define and evaluate the key events in the life and rule of Constantine
- To identify the lasting contributions of Rome

BUILDING BACKGROUND

Ask students to preview the chapter by reading the headings and subheadings, studying the photographs and captions, and examining the map. Based on the preview, work with students to compile a list of questions about the fall of Rome and the rise of Christianity. As students locate the answers to their questions, have them record them on the list.

VOCABULARY

empire huge region of varied cultures under the control of one government
citizen person owing loyalty to and entitled to protection by a state or a nation
Christianity the religion based on the life and teachings of Jesus Christ
convert person who has been convinced to change from one religion to another
barbarian name given to outsiders by the Romans, who viewed them as uncivilized
drought a long period of very low rainfall

As needed, have students consult the glossary to define the following words: *bishop, centralize, council, excommunicate, heretic, New Testament, persecution, plunder, saint*

WORKING WITH PRIMARY SOURCES

Point out the quotation from Ambrose on Student Edition page 23. If necessary, refer students to the glossary, and explain that excommunicated means to be deprived of the right of church membership by the church leadership. Discuss what the quotation reveals about early Christian beliefs. Why do you think Ambrose asked the emperor to repent? Invite students to read more of Ambrose's letter to the emperor, written in 390, at http://www.fordham.edu/halsall/source/ambrose-let51.html

CAST OF CHARACTERS

Augustine (aw-GUS-teen), Roman nobleman who converted to Christianity

Constantine the Great (KON-stun-teen), First Roman emperor to convert to Christianity

Visigoths (VIH-zih-goths), Arian Christian Germanic tribe that attacked Rome in 410

28   CHAPTER 1

WORKING WITH PRIMARY SOURCES

A major feature of *The Medieval & Early Modern World* is the opportunity to read about history through the words and images of the people who lived it. Each book includes excerpts from the best sources from these ancient civilizations, giving the narrative an immediacy that is difficult to match in secondary sources. Students can read further in these sources on their own or in small groups using the accompanying *Primary Sources and Reference Volume*. The Teaching Guide recommends activities so students of all skill levels can appreciate the ways people from the past saw themselves, their ideas and values, and their fears and dreams.

LINKING DISCIPLINES

Art Have students research examples of arches, roads, and aqueducts constructed throughout the Roman Empire. You might want to display a map of the Roman Empire on the wall. Instruct students to research in a library or on the Internet to find examples of Roman architecture. Have them sketch or print copies, write brief captions, and affix them on the map. Ask students to identify similarities between these ancient structures and familiar modern structures.

LITERACY TIPS

In addition to using the suggestions in the Supporting Learning and Extending Learning sections, refer back frequently to pages 20–23 for strategies and advice from a literacy coach.

WRITING

Persuasive Letter Have students review the events of Augustine's life as described in the chapter. Next have them write a persuasive letter or sermon that he might have addressed to non-Christians to describe his conversion and persuade them of his beliefs. What figurative language might he use to compel them? What experiences would he share from his life? (*Assessment: students incorporate supporting detail and language from the chapter. Their letters should also represent the tensions between Christians and non-Christians.*)

SUPPORTING LEARNING

English Language Learners Help students recognize and use multiple meaning words. Using the paragraphs on Student Edition page 27, identify and define such words as letters, beat, torn, and passage. Help students use context clues and their prior knowledge to figure out which meaning is being used. Ask volunteers to suggest sentences using various meanings of the words.

Struggling Readers Have students complete the Sequence of Events Chart at the back of the guide to show how one event led to another, and then another, in the history of early Christianity. For example, they can list how Christianity's spread led to the executions of Christians, and so on. Remind them to look for key dates, such as Constantine's conversion in 312.

EXTENDING LEARNING

Enrichment Invite students to learn more about one of these cities as they are today: Rome, Carthage, or Constantinople. Direct students to use search engines,

GEOGRAPHY CONNECTION

Movement Have students trace the routes of the Germanic migrations on the map on page 31. They may want to compare the map with a topographic map of Europe to locate features, such as mountains or rivers that either blocked or aided the movement of these peoples.

READING COMPREHENSION QUESTIONS

1. Why did economic and social conditions worsen in Rome? (*Rome depended on slaves to produce food. When the empire stopped expanding, it had fewer slaves to do the work.*)
2. Why did Roman authorities fear the early Christians? (*They worried about uprisings. Christianity was becoming popular among people who would likely rebel: the poor in cities, slaves, and soldiers.*)
3. Where did Constantine locate the new capital of the empire? (*Byzantium, a small Greek city near Asia Minor*)
4. Why did the Huns migrate west? (*Drought ruined their pasture, and they wanted better lives for themselves.*)
5. What happened after the Visigoths advanced on Rome in 410? (*The western emperor fled, and the Visigoths plundered Rome.*)

CRITICAL THINKING QUESTIONS

1. What does the image of the shield on Student Edition page 23 tell you about warfare during this time? (*Warfare included hand-to-hand combat. Soldiers had access to iron for added protection.*)
2. Why were the Romans, Germanic tribes, and Huns in conflict with each other? (*They wanted to either keep control of land and resources, or gain land and resources from the other groups. They fought rather than cooperate with each other.*)
3. One Goth observer described the Huns as "small, foul, and skinny." What does it say about the Goths' view of the Huns during this time? (*It shows their negative opinion of the Goths.*)

SOCIAL SCIENCES

Military History Attila the Hun is still famous today for his resilience and brutality. Have students research his attack on Rome using the Internet or library resources. Next have them use their history journals to write from Attila's point of view a series of short diary entries describing his advance toward Rome.

READING AND LANGUAGE ARTS

Reading Nonfiction As students read the text, have them use the strategy "list/group/label" to work with the vocabulary. First have them individually list words that relate to different cultures or religious groups as they read. Then have students form groups of three and share their lists. Next, ask the groups to identify and name at least five categories in which to put the words, and sort them into the categories to which they best belong. Finally, have each small group display their choices and share the reasons behind them with the class.

Using Language Direct students' attention to the quotation from Ambrose on page 27. Have them draw in their history journals an image it brings to mind. With partners, students can share images and discuss why Ambrose might have described the church the way he did. Next, have partners consider what the "raging sea" represents. As a whole class, speculate about the effect of his words on both Christians and on non-Christians.

THE EUROPEAN WORLD, 400–1450   29

WRITING

Each chapter has a suggestion for a specific writing assignment. These assignments can help students meet state requirements in writing as well improve their skills.

SUPPORTING LEARNING AND EXTENDING LEARNING

Suggestions for students of varying abilities and learning styles: advanced learners, struggling readers, auditory/visual/tactile learners, and English language learners. These may be individual, partner, or group activities. (For more on reading and literacy, see pp. 16–19.)

GEOGRAPHY CONNECTION

Each chapter has a Geography Connection to strengthen students' map skills as well as their understanding of how geography affects human civilization. One of the five themes of geography is highlighted in each chapter.

READING COMPREHENSION AND CRITICAL THINKING QUESTIONS

The reading comprehension questions are general enough to allow free-flowing class or small group discussion, yet specific enough to be used for oral or written assessment of students' grasp of the important information. The critical thinking questions are intended to engage students in a deeper analysis of the text and can also be used for oral or written assessment.

stretched 3,000 miles from east to west. Its capital was Rome. Today, Rome is the capital of Italy. Within Rome's borders lies Vatican City, a sovereign state and the residence of the Pope, the leader of the Roman Catholic Church.

SOCIAL SCIENCES ACTIVITIES

These activities connect the subject matter in the Student Edition with economics, civics, and science, technology, and society.

READING AND LANGUAGE ARTS

Some activities can facilitate the development of nonfiction reading strategies. Others help students' appreciation of fiction and poetry, focusing on word choice, description, and figurative language.

Icons quickly help identify key concepts, facts, activities, and assessment activities in the sidebars.

▶ Cast of Characters
This sidebar points out and identifies significant personalities in the chapter. Pronunciation guides are included where necessary.

▶ Then and Now
This feature provides interesting facts and ideas about the ancient civilization and relates it to the modern world. This may be an aspect of government still in use today, word origins of common modern expressions, physical reminders of the past, and other features. You can use this item simply to promote interest in the subject matter or as a springboard to other research.

▶ Linking Disciplines
This feature offers opportunities to investigate other subject areas that relate to the material in the Student Edition: math, science, arts, and health. Specific areas of these subjects are emphasized: **Math** (arithmetic, algebra, geometry, data, statistics); **Science** (life science, earth science, physical science); **Arts** (music, arts, dance, drama, architecture); **Health** (personal health, world health).

▶ For Homework
A quick glance links you to additional activities in the Student Study Guide that can be assigned as homework.

ASSESSMENT

The Medieval & Early Modern World program intentionally omits from the Student Edition the kinds of section, chapter, and unit questions that are used to review and assess learning in standard textbooks. It is the purpose of the series to engage readers in learning—and loving—history written as good literature. Rather than interrupting student reading and enjoyment, all assessment instruments for the series have been placed in the Teaching Guides.

► CHAPTER TESTS

A reproducible chapter test follows each chapter in this Teaching Guide. These tests will help you assess students' mastery of the content addressed in each chapter. These tests measure a variety of cognitive and analytical skills, particularly comprehension, critical thinking, and expository writing through multiple choice, short answer, and essay questions.
An answer key for the chapter tests is provided at the end of the Teaching Guide.

► WRAP-UP TEST

After the last chapter test you will find a wrap-up test consisting of 10 essay questions that evaluate students' ability to synthesize and express what they've learned about the civilization under study. Depending upon your class, you may want to consider assigning the questions as a takehome or open-book test.

► RUBRICS

The rubrics at the back of this Teaching Guide will help you assess students' written work, oral presentations, and group projects. They include a Scoring Rubric based on standards for good writing and effective cooperative learning. In addition, a simplified hand-out is provided, plus a form for evaluating group projects and a Library/Media Center Research Log to help students focus and evaluate their research. Students can also evaluate their own work using these rubrics.

► BLACKLINE MASTERS (BLMs)

Two blackline masters follow each chapter in the Teaching Guide. These BLMs are reproducible pages for you to use as in-class activities or homework exercises. Assigning primary source blackline masters to groups or partners is strongly encouraged, as this material may be quite challenging to some students. They can also be used for assessment as needed.

► ADDITIONAL ASSESSMENT ACTIVITIES

The Group Project sections and Chapter Lessons of this Teaching Guide provide numerous activities and projects that have been designated as additional assessment opportunities, using the rubrics at the back of this Guide.

USING THE STUDENT STUDY GUIDE FOR ASSESSMENT

► Study Guide Activities
  Assignments in the Student Study Guide correspond with those in the Teaching Guide. If needed, these Student Study Guide activities can be used for assessment.

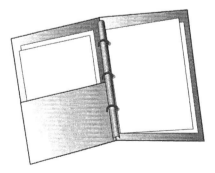

► Portfolio Approach
  Student Study Guide pages can be removed from the workbook and turned in for grading. When the pages are returned, they can be part of the students' individual history journals. Have students keep a 3-ring binder portfolio of Study Guide pages alongside writing projects and other activities.

STUDENT STUDY GUIDE: **KEY FEATURES**

The Student Study Guide works as both standalone instructional material and as a support to the Student Edition and this Teaching Guide. Certain activities encourage informal small-group or family participation. These features make it an effective teaching tool:

Flexibility

You can use the Study Guide in the classroom, with individuals or small groups, or send it home for homework. You can distribute the entire guide to students; however, the pages are perforated so you can remove and distribute only the pertinent lessons.

A page on reports and special projects directs students to the "Further Reading" resource in the student edition. This feature gives students general guidance on doing research and devising independent study projects of their own.

FACSIMILE SPREAD

The Study Guide begins with a facsimile spread from the Student Edition. This spread gives reading strategies and highlights key features: captions, primary sources, sidebars, headings, etymologies. The spread supplies the contextualization students need to fully understand the material.

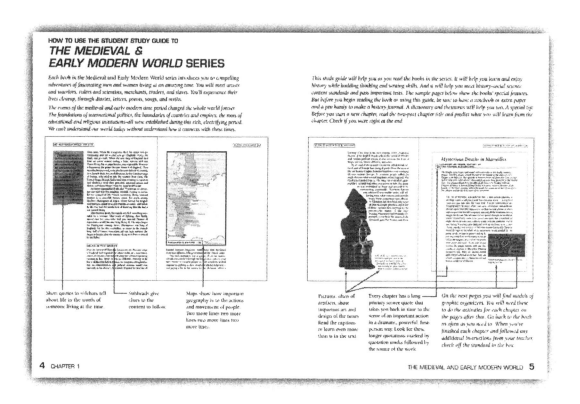

Portfolio Approach

The Study Guide pages are three-hole-punched so they can be integrated with notebook paper in a looseleaf binder. This history journal or portfolio can become both a record of content mastery and an outlet for each student's unique creative expression. Responding to prompts, students can write poetry or songs, plays and character sketches, create storyboards or cartoons, or construct multi-layered timelines.

The portfolio approach gives students unlimited opportunities for practice in areas that need strengthening. Students can share their journals and compare their work. And the Study Guide pages in the portfolio make a valuable assessment tool for you. The portfolio is an ongoing record of performance that can be reviewed and graded periodically.

GRAPHIC ORGANIZERS

This feature contains reduced models of seven graphic organizers referenced frequently in the study guide. Using these devices will help students organize the material so it is meaningful to them. (Full-size reproducibles of each graphic organizer are provided at the back of this Teaching Guide.) These graphic organizers include: outline, main idea map, K-W-L chart (What I Know, What I Want to Know, What I Learned), Venn diagram, timeline, sequence of events chart, and T-chart.

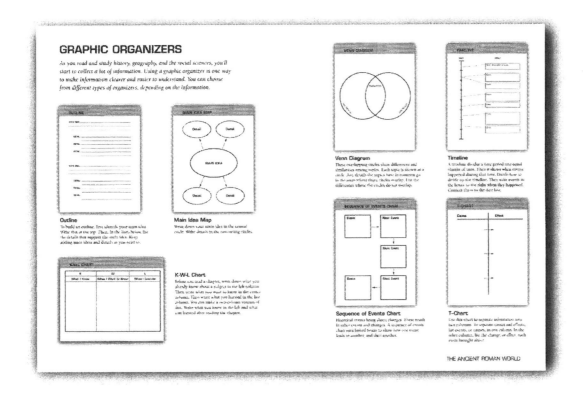

Each chapter lesson is designed to draw students into the subject matter. Recurring features and exercises challenge their knowledge and allow them to practice valuable analysis and English language arts skills. Activities in the Teaching Guide and Student Study Guide complement but do not duplicate each other. Together they offer a wide range of class work, group projects, and opportunities for further study and assessment that can be tailored to all ability levels.

CHAPTER SUMMARY
briefly reviews big ideas from the chapter.

ACCESS
invites students into the content by building background, tapping prior knowledge, or visual note-taking.

CAST OF CHARACTERS
reintroduces key personalities from the Student Edition

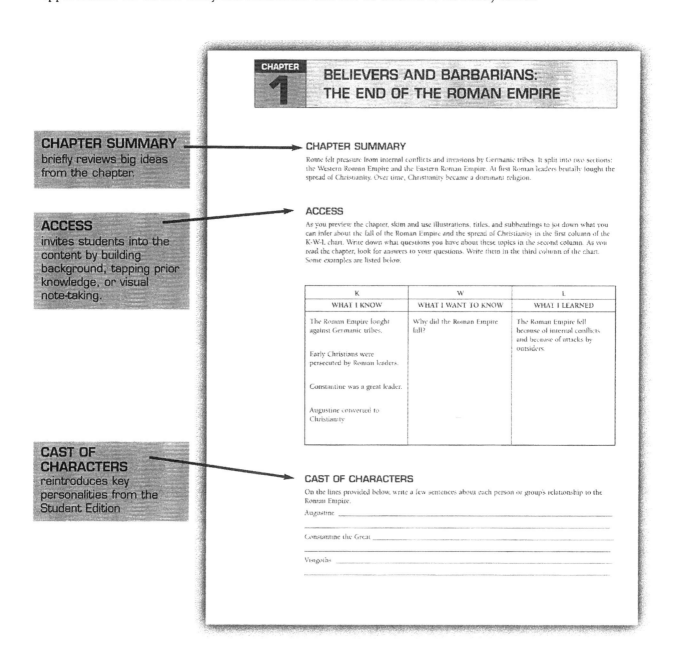

CHAPTER 1

BELIEVERS AND BARBARIANS: THE END OF THE ROMAN EMPIRE

CHAPTER SUMMARY

Rome felt pressure from internal conflicts and invasions by Germanic tribes. It split into two sections: the Western Roman Empire and the Eastern Roman Empire. At first Roman leaders brutally fought the spread of Christianity. Over time, Christianity became a dominant religion.

ACCESS

As you preview the chapter, skim and use illustrations, titles, and subheadings to jot down what you can infer about the fall of the Roman Empire and the spread of Christianity in the first column of the K-W-L chart. Write down what questions you have about these topics in the second column. As you read the chapter, look for answers to your questions. Write them in the third column of the chart. Some examples are listed below.

K	W	L
WHAT I KNOW	WHAT I WANT TO KNOW	WHAT I LEARNED
The Roman Empire fought against Germanic tribes.	Why did the Roman Empire fall?	The Roman Empire fell because of internal conflicts and because of attacks by outsiders.
Early Christians were persecuted by Roman leaders.		
Constantine was a great leader.		
Augustine converted to Christianity.		

CAST OF CHARACTERS

On the lines provided below, write a few sentences about each person or group's relationship to the Roman Empire.

Augustine _____

_____

Constantine the Great _____

_____

Visigoths _____

_____

WORD BANK
Choose five of the six words below and use them to write a paragraph about the Roman Empire in your history journal.

1. (empire, citizen)
2. (Christianity, convert)
3. (barbarian, drought)

WORD PLAY
Look up the word *citizen* in the dictionary. Find out its origin. Explain how the word's original meaning relates to its current meaning.

WITH A PARENT OR PARTNER
One of the forces of Germanic migration was a drought in the fourth century. With a parent or partner, research other famous or catastrophic droughts from another time period in history. Create and illustrate a chart that contrasts life in the area, community, or culture before and after the drought. Display your chart in the classroom.

CRITICAL THINKING
CONTRASTING CULTURES
The end of the Roman Empire saw two cultures—the old culture of the Romans, the Christians, and the barbarians clashed...
contrasts include: how...

CONTRAST
The ancient Roman religious belief in many gods. Christianity based on the belief in one...

Look at pages 28 and 29 in...
Roman/Mediterranean cult...
details for each culture. Th...
partner.

Category
Environment

WORKING WITH PRIMARY SOURCES
Read the law of the Franks, a Germanic people, on Student Edition page 29.

> If anyone has assaulted and plundered a free person, and it be proved against him, he shall be [fined] 2,500 denars, which make 63 shillings. If a Roman has plundered a Frank... above law shall be observed. But if a Frank has plundered a Roman, he shall be [fined] 35 shillings.

IDENTIFYING POINT OF VIEW
The first Germanic kings copied the Roman practice of writing codes of law. In the late 400s, for example, King Euric, the Visigoth king of Gaul, wrote the Germanic customary law into code.

1. What crimes does the law address?
_____

2. Why do you think customary laws, or laws based on tradition and custom, were eventually written down?
_____

3. What does the law show about the Franks' attitudes toward the Romans at this time?
_____

4. Do you know of any other laws in history that showed bias toward one group of people in a society? Give examples.
_____

WRITE ABOUT IT
In your history journal, write an essay in which you invent a rule or law for your community, family, or school that you believe would improve the quality of life for everyone. Write about why...

ALL OVER THE MAP
Directions: Follow the steps below to complete the map.

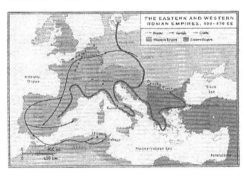

THE EASTERN AND WESTERN ROMAN EMPIRES, 400–470 CE

- Scan pages 28–32 to find information on the migrations of the Franks, Vandals, Visigoths, and the Huns.
- Look on a physical-political map of modern Europe and Asia in an atlas.
- Write the mountain ranges on the map here.
- Label the Balkan Peninsula.
- Label Central Asia.
- Draw a line showing the approximate migration route of the Huns.
- Add the line representing the Huns and the term *Huns* to the key.
- Write a paragraph in your history journal that answers these questions:
  - What were the natural boundaries of the Roman Empire's northern frontier?
  - What physical features affected the migrations of each group?
- Give your map a title that explains what the map shows.

WORD BANK
reintroduces key curricular terms and difficult words from the Student Edition.

CRITICAL THINKING
exercises draw on such thinking skills as establishing cause and effect, making inferences, comparing and contrasting, identifying main ideas and details, and other analytical process.

WORKING WITH PRIMARY SOURCES
invites students to read primary sources closely. Exercises include DBQ's, evaluating point of view, and writing.

WRITE ABOUT IT
A writing assignment may stem from a vocabulary word, a historical event, or a primary source. The assignment can be a newspaper article, letter, short essay, a scene with dialogue, a diary entry.

ALL OVER THE MAP
uses engaging map skills activities to help students understand geography's crucial role in shaping history.

The books in this series are written in a lively, narrative style to inspire a love of reading history. English language learners and struggling readers are given special consideration within the program's exercises and activities. And students who love to read and learn will also benefit from the program's rich and varied material. Following are strategies to make sure each and every student gets the most out of the subjects you will teach through *The Medieval & Early Modern World*.

ENGLISH LANGUAGE LEARNERS

For English learners to achieve academic success, the instructional considerations for teachers include two mandates:

- Help them attain grade level, content area knowledge, and academic language.
- Provide for the development of English language proficiency.

To accomplish these goals, you should plan lessons that reflect the student's level of English proficiency. Students progress through five developmental levels as they increase in language proficiency:

Beginning and Early Intermediate *(grade level material will be mostly incomprehensible, students need a great deal of teacher support)*

Intermediate *(grade level work will be a challenge)*

Early Advanced and Advanced *(close to grade level reading and writing, students continue to need support)*

Refer to your state's ELD Standards for information about language proficiency at each level. The books in this program are written at the intermediate level. However, you can still use the lesson plans for students of different levels by using the strategies below:

Tap Prior Knowledge
What students know about the topic will help determine your next steps for instruction. Using K-W-L charts, brainstorming, and making lists are ways to find out what they know. English learners bring a rich cultural diversity into the classroom. By sharing what they know, students can connect their knowledge and experiences to the course.

Set the Context
Use different tools to make new information understandable. These can be images, artifacts, maps, timelines, illustrations, charts, videos, or graphic organizers. Techniques such as role-playing and story-boarding can also be helpful. Speak in shorter sentences, with careful enunciation, expanded explanations, repetitions, and paraphrasing. Use fewer idiomatic expressions.

Show—Don't Just Tell
English learners often get lost as they listen to directions, explanations, lectures, and discussions. By showing students what is expected, you can help them participate more fully in classroom activities. Students need to be shown how to use the graphic organizers in this guide and the mini versions in the student study guide, as well as other blackline masters for note-taking and practice. An overhead transparency with whole or small groups is also effective.

Use the Text

Because of unfamiliar words, students will need help. Teach them to preview the chapter using text features (headings, bold print, sidebars, italics). See the suggestions in the facsimile of the Student Edition, shown on pages 6–7 of the Student Study Guide. Show students organizing structures such as cause and effect or comparing and contrasting. Have students read to each other in pairs. Encourage them to share their history journals with each other. Use Read Aloud/Think Aloud, perhaps with an overhead transparency. Help them create word banks, charts, and graphic organizers. Discuss the main idea after reading.

Check for Understanding

Rather than simply ask students if they understand, stop frequently and ask them to paraphrase or expand on what you just said. Such techniques will give you a much clearer assessment of their understanding.

Provide for Interaction

As students interact with the information and speak their thoughts, their content knowledge and academic language skills improve. Increase interaction in the classroom through cooperative learning, small group work, and partner share. By working and talking with others, students can practice asking and answering questions.

Use Appropriate Assessment

When modifying the instruction, you will also need to modify the assessment. Multiple choice, true and false, and other criterion reference tests are suitable, but consider changing test format and structure. English learners are constantly improving their language proficiency in their oral and written responses, but they are often grammatically incorrect. Remember to be thoughtful and fair about giving students credit for their content knowledge and use of academic language, even if their English isn't perfect.

STRUGGLING READERS

Some students struggle to understand the information presented in a textbook. The following strategies for content-area reading can help students improve their ability to make comparisons, sequence events, determine importance, summarize, evaluate, synthesize, analyze, and solve problems.

Build Knowledge of Genre

Both the fiction and narrative nonfiction genres are incorporated into *The Medieval & Early Modern World*. This combination of genres makes the text interesting and engaging. But teachers must be sure students can identify and use the organizational structures of both genres.

Fiction	Nonfiction
Each chapter is a story	Content: historical information
Setting: historical time and place	Organizational structure: cause/effect, sequence of events, problem/solution
Characters: historical figures	Other features: maps, timelines, sidebars, photographs, primary sources
Plot: problems, roadblocks, and resolutions	

In addition, the textbook has a wealth of the text features of nonfiction: bold and italic print, sidebars, headings and subheadings, labels, captions, and "signal words" such as *first*, *next*, and *finally*. Teaching these organizational structures and text features is essential for struggling readers.

Build Background

Having background information about a topic makes reading about it so much easier. When students lack background information, teachers can preteach or "front load" concepts and vocabulary, using a variety of instructional techniques. Conduct a chapter or book walk, looking at titles, headings, and other text features to develop a big picture of the content. Focus on new vocabulary words during the "walk" and create a word bank with illustrations for future reference. Read aloud key passages and discuss the meaning. Focus on the timeline and maps to help students develop a sense of time and place. Show a video, go to a website, and have trade books and magazines on the topic available for student exploration.

Comprehension Strategies

While reading, successful readers are predicting, making connections, monitoring, visualizing, questioning, inferring, and summarizing. Struggling readers have a harder time with these "in the head" processes. The following strategies will help these students construct meaning from the text until they are able to do it on their own.

PREDICT: Before reading, conduct a picture and text feature "tour" of the chapter to make predictions. Ask students if they remember if this has ever happened before, to predict what might happen this time.

MAKE CONNECTIONS: Help students relate content to their background (text to text, text to self, and text to the world).

MONITOR AND CONFIRM: Encourage students to stop reading when they come across an unknown word, phrase, or concept. In their notebooks, have them make a note of text they don't understand and ask for clarification or figure it out. While this activity slows down reading at first, it is effective in improving skills over time.

VISUALIZE: Students benefit from imagining the events described in a story. Sketching scenes, story-boarding, role-playing, and looking for sensory details all help students with this strategy.

INFER: Help students look beyond the literal meaning of a text to understand deeper meanings. Graphic organizers and discussions provide opportunities to broaden their understanding. Looking closely at the "why" of historical events helps students infer.

QUESTION AND DISCUSS: Have students jot down their questions as they read, and then share them during discussions. Or have students come up with the type of questions they think a teacher would ask. Over time students will develop more complex inferential questions, which lead to group discussions. Questioning and discussing also helps students see ideas from multiple perspectives and draw conclusions, both critical skills for understanding history.

DETERMINE IMPORTANCE: Teach students how to decide what is most important from all the facts and details in nonfiction. After reading for an overall understanding, they can go back to highlight important ideas, words, and phrases. Clues for determining importance include bold or italic print, signal words, and other text features. A graphic organizer such as a main idea map also helps.

Teach and Practice Decoding Strategies

Rather than simply defining an unfamiliar word, teach struggling readers decoding strategies:

- Have them look at the prefix, suffix, and root to help figure out the new word.

- Look for words they know within the word.

- Use the context for clues, and read further or reread.

ADVANCED LEARNERS

Every classroom has students who finish the required assignments and then want additional challenges. Fortunately, the very nature of history and social science offers a wide range of opportunities for students to explore topics in greater depth. Encourage them to come up with their own ideas for an additional assignment. Determine the final product, its presentation, and a timeline for completion.

► Research

Students can develop in-depth understanding through seeking information, exploring ideas, asking and answering questions, making judgments, considering points of view, and evaluating actions and events. They will need access to a wide range of resource materials: the Internet, maps, encyclopedias, trade books, magazines, dictionaries, artifacts, newspapers, museum catalogues, brochures, and the library. See the "Further Reading" section at the end of the Student Edition for good jumping-off points.

► Projects

You can encourage students to capitalize on their strengths as learners (visual, verbal, kinesthetic, or musical) or to try a new way of responding. Students can prepare a debate or write a persuasive paper, play, skit, poem, song, dance, game, puzzle, or biography. They can create an alphabet book on the topic, film a video, do a book talk, or illustrate a book. They can render charts, graphs, or other visual representations. Allow for creativity and support students' thinking.

Cheryl A. Caldera, M.A.
Literacy Coach

GROUP PROJECTS

These interactive, multimedia projects give every student the chance to experience some aspect of life in *An Age of Empires, 1200–1750*. They will add fun and depth to your exploration of this amazing time in history and can be used for assessment with the rubrics at the back of this Teaching Guide.

Chapter 1
▶ Drama

Invite students to work in small groups to write a script and design costumes, scenery, and props for a play about the life of Genghis Khan. Encourage students to use information from the chapter as well as other nonfiction resources. You may wish to suggest that different groups focus on different time periods of Genghis Khan's life. For example, one group may write a short play about his childhood, another about events when he was a young adult and becoming Khan, and a third about his military exploits as Khan. Allow the groups time to prepare and present their plays.

As an additional assessment for this dramatic presentation, use the Group Project rubric at the back of this guide. Have students rate their own work with the self-assessment rubric.

Chapter 2
▶ Military Tactics and Geography

Invite small groups of students to investigate the geographic challenges faced by Mongol armies as they planned their military strategies to conquer an enemy. Have students scan the chapter for Mongol conquests and other battles, and have each group choose one site as their focus. Tell each group to plan a presentation on the advantages and disadvantages the Mongols had in the encounter. For example, students might cite a grassland area as an advantage for Mongol horses, while steep mountains or vast deserts are probably disadvantages. Suggest that each group include a topographical map, along with other visuals in their presentations.

As an additional assessment for the presentations, use the Group Project rubric at the back of this guide. Have students rate their own work with the self-assessment rubric.

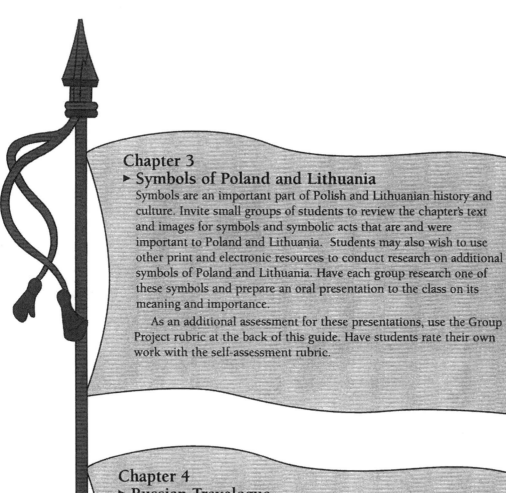

Chapter 3
▶ Symbols of Poland and Lithuania

Symbols are an important part of Polish and Lithuanian history and culture. Invite small groups of students to review the chapter's text and images for symbols and symbolic acts that are and were important to Poland and Lithuania. Students may also wish to use other print and electronic resources to conduct research on additional symbols of Poland and Lithuania. Have each group research one of these symbols and prepare an oral presentation to the class on its meaning and importance.

As an additional assessment for these presentations, use the Group Project rubric at the back of this guide. Have students rate their own work with the self-assessment rubric.

Chapter 4
▶ Russian Travelogue

Have students work in small groups to plan an imaginary trip to see tsarist Russia. Suggest that groups revisit the chapter to note cities and unique buildings that would be worth seeing. Then, have them use maps to plan their trips. Have each group present their travel plans to the class using visuals such as maps and photographs of sites to be visited. If groups decided to omit any sites from their travelogues, have them explain their reasoning.

As an additional assessment for the travelogues, use the Group Project rubric at the back of this guide. Have students rate their own work with the self-assessment rubric.

Chapter 5
▶ Mughal Museum

Have students work in small groups to create exhibits for a Mughal Museum. Each group should agree on a topic, research it, and come to an agreement about what to include in their display. Direct groups to assign specific tasks to each member.

Encourage students to be creative in their presentations. They might, for example, create posters, scale models, or diagrams of buildings such as the Taj Mahal, the Jami Mosque, or the Red Fort. They might prepare a visual history of the Koh-i-Nor diamond. Groups who decide to report on Mughal leaders might enjoy creating Mughal Mogols profiles. Provide classroom time for oral presentations of each exhibit.

As an additional assessment, use the Group Project rubric at the back of this guide to evaluate each exhibit. Have students rate their own work with the self-assessment rubric.

Chapter 6
▶ Ottoman IQ

Invite groups of students to create an Ottoman game show, in which contestants win points for their knowledge of the empire, its rulers, and its customs. Each group may decide on their game's format and rules, and should develop a set of questions for contestants to answer. Have a volunteer from each group give an overview of their game, and then allow time for contestants to compete in each format.

Use the Group Project rubric at the back of this guide to assess students' understanding of the Ottoman Empire. Have students rate their own work with the self-assessment rubric.

Chapter 7
▶ Chronology

Have students create a timeline and map that show events in the expansion of the Ottoman Empire. You may wish to have students include events from Chapter 6 as well. Students may use numbers, letters, or icons to show corresponding events on the timeline and map. Encourage students to conduct additional research to include at least one event that is not discussed in the Student Edition.

As an additional assessment for this chronology, use the Group Project rubric at the back of this guide. Have students rate their own work with the self-assessment rubric.

Chapter 8
▶ Gallery of Portuguese Explorers

Invite students to prepare a Gallery of Portuguese Explorers. Assign students to work in small groups, and have each group research a different Portuguese explorer. Instruct each group to write a brief illustrated biography of the explorer and to make a map that shows the explorer's voyages of discovery. Biographies should explain the effects of the explorer's discoveries, including the establishment of trade routes and the products and inventions that traveled along these routes. Have groups work together to create a classroom timeline about the explorer's lives, and to arrange their work in a Gallery of Portuguese Explorers.

As an additional assessment for this activity, use the Group Project rubric at the back of this guide. Have students rate their own work with the self-assessment rubric.

Chapter 9
▶ Drama: The Decision to Fund Columbus's Voyage

Ask small groups of students to dramatize a conversation between Queen Isabella and the naval committee about whether to fund Columbus's first voyage. One student should role-play Christopher Columbus, as he presents his case. Encourage them to use information from the chapter and from additional research. Suggest that they consider the possible outcomes of different decisions before arriving at their final choice.

Use the Group Project rubric at the back of this guide to assess students' understanding of the challenges Columbus faced in getting approval for his explorations. Have students rate their own work with the self-assessment rubric.

Chapter 10
▶ Matchmaker, Matchmaker

Have pairs of students work together to research one of the Habsburg marriages or families during the empire's 500-year reign. Students should aim to determine the role the marriage or family played within the empire, and examine its strengths and weaknesses. Students should create a visual display that illustrates their findings, and present it to the class in an oral report.

As an additional assessment, use the Group Project rubric at the back of this guide to evaluate partners' displays. Have students rate their own work with the self-assessment rubric.

Chapter 11
▶ Imperial Press Conference

Have groups of students plan and conduct press conferences in which newspaper reporters interview Manchu leaders of China. Groups should review chapter content, and conduct additional research as needed. Remind students that Qing leaders saw themselves as ideal leaders who ruled firmly to benefit their people. "Reporters" and "rulers" should show appropriate respect during the questioning process, while discussing the rulers' decisions, mistakes, or personal flaws.

As an additional assessment for this activity, use the Group Project rubric at the back of this guide. Have students rate their own work with the self-assessment rubric.

CHAPTER 1

GOLDEN KHAN, GOLDEN REINS, GOLDEN HORDE: THE MONGOLS RIDE OUT PAGES 16-26

FOR HOMEWORK

STUDENT STUDY GUIDE

pages 11–14

CHAPTER SUMMARY

In 1206 the Mongol clans of Central Asia established Temujin as their leader, Genghis Khan. His disciplined army, le0d by talented and loyal generals, used proven military tactics to create an empire that stretched from Korea to central Europe. The Mongols caused much destruction, yet also made improvements to the Silk Road that restored international trade as they created the largest land empire in the world.

PERFORMANCE OBJECTIVES

- ▶ To explain the significance of Genghis Khan and other Mongol leaders
- ▶ To identify factors that made the Mongols successful in building an empire
- ▶ To identify the destruction and the improvements made by the Mongols
- ▶ To understand the importance of trade between China and other civilizations in the Mongol empire

BUILDING BACKGROUND

Ask students to suggest resources and skills that leaders need in order to build an empire. As needed, prompt students by suggesting things such as wise advisors and a well-trained military. List suggestions on a chart. Then tell students that they are going to read about how the Mongol empire was formed.

CAST OF CHARACTERS

Batu (bah-TOO) Mongol leader of Golden Horde controlling Russia

Genghis Khan (GENG-guhs KAHN) leader who led Mongols in forming the largest land empire

Khubilai Khan (KOO-buh-lie KAHN) Mongol ruler of China in Yuan Dynasty

Polo, Marco merchant who traveled to China during Khubilai Khan's era

VOCABULARY

conquered defeated by force

maneuvers movements that involve skill or cunning

campaign a series of military operations during a war

brutality cruelty, ruthlessness

invincibility the condition of being undefeatable

coalition an alliance formed for a particular purpose

ambush a surprise attack made from a concealed position

As needed, have students consult the glossary to define the following words: *gers, shaman.*

WORKING WITH PRIMARY SOURCES

Point out the quotation from Genghis Khan at the end of the first paragraph on Student Edition page 20. Discuss what the quotation reveals about Genghis Khan's perception of his troops and of his enemies. Ask students to state in their own words how Genghis Khan expected his troops to behave. Discuss what the references to animals reveal about Mongol life.

GEOGRAPHY CONNECTION

Location Have students locate Karakorum on the map on Student Edition page 17. Discuss the advantages of Karakorum's location as a base for invading China, and the city's possible disadvantages as a base for invading Kiev.

READING COMPREHENSION QUESTIONS

1. For what things did the Mongols rely on their horses? (*transportation, hunting, food, quick maneuvering*)
2. Why was winter the time of year that Genghis Khan preferred to start wars? (*Other nations did not expect attacks during the winter. The Mongol horse made it possible for the Mongols to attack in winter because it could withstand blizzards and dig through snow to find food.*)
3. What reasons might Genghis Khan have had for deciding to conquer Asia? (*He may have wanted the clans to fight others so they would not fight one another. He may have wanted China's wealth and iron. He may simply have enjoyed fighting.*)
4. What happened to the Mongol empire after Genghis Khan died? (*It was increasingly split up into sections with different sons and grandsons ruling.*)
5. What does the author suggest balanced the destruction caused by the Mongols? (*the increase in trade that resulted after the Mongols gained power*)
6. What was the purpose of the Mongols' tactic of pretending to give up and retreat from a battle? (*By pretending to give up, the Mongols fooled the enemy army into coming outside the protective walls of their cities. The Mongols were then able to ambush the unsuspecting enemy.*)

CRITICAL THINKING QUESTIONS

1. Why do you think that the clans established Temujin as their leader? (*He showed military cunning and leadership ability when he virtually wiped out the Tartars and defeated other clans that had wronged him or his family.*)
2. How might Temujin's life have been different if the Tartars hadn't killed his father? (*Temujin's childhood may have been easier. He wouldn't have needed to avenge his father's death and probably wouldn't have wiped out the Tartars; thus, Temujin may not have been established as Khan or guided the Mongols in building an empire.*)
3. What were some positive aspects of Mongol society? (*The Mongols were tolerant of religious ideas. Some leadership roles existed for women. Their custom encouraged people to give one of every 100 sheep to charity, and some of the goods they took in raids were given to children whose fathers had been killed.*)

SOCIAL SCIENCES

Economics Remind students that reports of the use of paper money in China surprised Europeans. Have students learn more about the history of money—including its functions and standards of value—and the economy in China during Mongol rule. Have students take notes and prepare an oral report to share their findings.

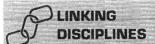

THEN and NOW

Genghis Khan established his headquarters at Karakorum in 1220. Archaeologists discovered the ruins of the abandoned city in 1889. Today visitors can tour a former Buddhist monastery built upon the site in the late 1500s.

LINKING DISCIPLINES

Art Have students research the *gers*, or yurt, the traditional round tents in which Mongols lived. Suggest that students draw and label the parts of a *gers*, describe its features, and tell whether it is still used today, and why.

There are numerous enjoyable books that will broaden students' knowledge of the rise of the Mongol Empire.

Carpini, Giovanni di Plano. *The Story of the Mongols Whom We Call the Tartars: Friar Giovanni di Plano Carpini's Account of His Embassy to the Court of the Mongol Khan.* Branden Books, 1996. Nonfiction. A friar sent by the pope to learn more about the Mongols provided this first-person account. ADVANCED

Dion, Frederick. *The Blue Wolf: The Epic Tale of the Life of Genghis Khan and the Empire of the Steppes.* Thomas Dunne Books, 2003. Historical Fiction. This story focuses on Genghis Khan's rise to power. ADVANCED

Khan, Paul. *Secret History of the Mongols: The Origin of Chingis Khan.* Cheng & Tsui, 1999. Poetry. Based on a translation, this narrative poem gives the Mongols' perspective on the rise of their nation. AVERAGE

LITERACY TIPS

In addition to using the suggestions in the Supporting Learning and Extending Learning sections, refer back frequently to pages 16–19 for strategies and advice from a literacy coach.

READING AND LANGUAGE ARTS

Reading Nonfiction   As students read Chapter 1, direct them to note and list details about the Mongol military and Mongol society in a two-column chart. After reading, encourage students to use the details they listed in their chart to draw conclusions about the Mongol military and society. Use this activity to assess students' understanding of key features of the Mongol Empire.

Using Language   Identify the simile in the second paragraph on Student Edition page 16. Explain that a simile is a figure of speech that often uses like or as to compare two unlike things. Restate the sentence as follows: *The Mongols destroyed many civilizations.* Discuss which sentence is more effective and why. Have students note and discuss other examples of figurative language in Chapter 1.

WRITING

Explanation   Have students use information from Chapter 1 to write an essay that explains why Genghis Khan was a skilled military commander. Before students write, suggest that they list details about Genghis Khan's childhood that shaped his character and about his military strategies.

SUPPORTING LEARNING

English Language Learners   Before students read, identify and clarify the meaning of multiple-meaning words, such as *spent, driving, hard,* and *drive* (Student Edition page 19). Have students list multiple-meaning words in a personal dictionary.

Struggling Readers   Guide students to create a three-column chart to list details that describe *Mongol Horses, The Mongol People,* and *Genghis Khan.* After students read the chapter, have them use the details listed in their chart to summarize why Mongol horses, the Mongol people, and Genghis Khan were tough.

EXTENDING LEARNING

Enrichment   Invite students to role-play a military planning session between Genghis Khan and one or more of his generals. Tell them to scan the chapter for information about Mongol tactics and to use the ideas in the conversation.

Extension   Direct students' attention to the Mongol proverb in the second complete paragraph on Student Edition page 22. Invite students to work with a partner to make up sayings that could be applied to Mongol life. Allow time for students to share and discuss their sayings.

NAME _____ **DATE** _____

MONGOL CONQUEST, 1260

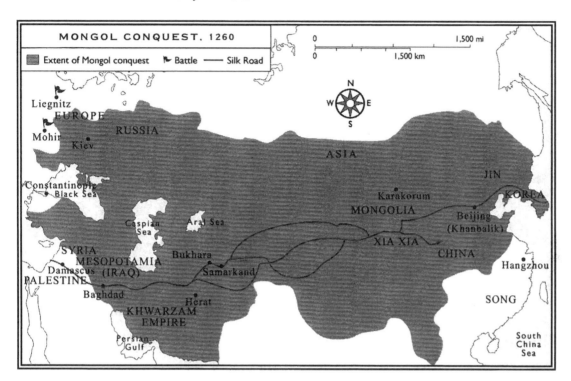

Directions

Use the map to answer the questions that follow.

1. What does the map show?

_____

2. About how many miles apart were the easternmost and the westernmost Mongol conquests? Use the scale of miles to calculate the approximate distance.

_____

3. Which cities shown on the map were part of the Mongol conquest?

_____

4. What cities lay outside the area of Mongol conquest as of 1260?

_____

5. Which Chinese dynasty was not yet part of the Mongol conquest?

_____

NAME _____   DATE _____

TO THE VICTOR GO THE SPOILS

Directions

The following quotations appear on Student Edition pages 19 and 24. Read the quotations and answer the questions that follow. Use a separate sheet of paper if necessary.

> It is my intention that your wives and daughters shall be dressed in gold embroidered dresses, ride quiet geldings, and have clean and pleasant tasting water to drink, [and] your herds shall have good pastures.
>
> —Genghis Khan to his bodyguards

> We came across countless skulls and bones of dead men lying about the ground. Kiev had been a very large and thickly populated town, but now it has been reduced almost to nothing.
>
> —John of Plano Carpini

1. How do the things Genghis Khan promised to his bodyguards show what was important in life for a Mongol?

_____

_____

_____

_____

2. Based on what you read in Chapter 1, what happened to Genghis Khan's enemies?

_____

_____

_____

3. Why do you think Genghis Khan promises to care for the needs of the bodyguard's families, rather than for the guards themselves?

_____

_____

_____

4. Based on what you read in Chapter 1, what can you infer about what the people of Kiev did when they realized Genghis Khan's soldiers were about to attack?

_____

_____

_____

5. What might explain the contrast between what the Mongol leader believed his own people deserved, and what the Mongols believed their enemies deserved?

_____

_____

_____

A. COMPREHENSION

Circle the letter of the best answer for each question.

1. What was the extent of the territory conquered by the Mongols?
   a. from Japan to Hungary
   b. from southeast Asia to Scandinavia
   c. all of Asia
   d. from Korea to central Europe

2. What did the Mongols usually do after a city surrendered without a fight?
   a. The Mongols burned the city.
   b. They took goods and weapons but allowed people and buildings to survive.
   c. Mongols enslaved the citizens and then moved into the city themselves.
   d. Mongol generals showed little mercy on the city and its citizens.

3. Which of the following was probably not a reason why Genghis Khan decided to conquer all of Asia?
   a. He wanted Mongol clans to be busy.
   b. He hoped to control the seas around Asia as well as the land.
   c. He wanted China's wealth and iron.
   d. He enjoyed fighting.

4. What advantage did the Mongols see in destroying cities?
   a. It created open land for pastures.
   b. It allowed them to rebuild cities in the Mongol style.
   c. They believed it prevented conquered people from organizing a rebellion.
   d. They thought the land could be used to imprison the conquered people.

B. SEQUENCE OF EVENTS

Write two or three sentences to answer each question.

5. What did the Mongols do after they chose a target? _____

   _____

6. Where did the Mongols focus their fighting at the start of a battle? _____

   _____

7. What did the Mongols do if they couldn't break through their target's defenses? _____

   _____

C. SUPPORTING AN OPINION

On Student Edition page 24, the author states that "Some of the destruction of the Mongols was balanced by the increase in trade." Based on what you have read about the Mongols, do you agree with the author's statement? On a separate sheet of paper, write one or more paragraphs explaining your answer. Use details from the chapter to support your opinion.

FOR HOMEWORK

**STUDENT
STUDY GUIDE**

pages 15–18

**CAST OF
CHARACTERS**

Genghis Khan
(Temujin) (GENG-guhs
KHAN) Mongol
conqueror of largest
land empire

Marco Polo Venetian
merchant who traveled
to China during Khubilai
Khan's era

Khubilai Khan (KOO-
buh-lie KHAN) Mongol
ruler of China in Yuan
Dynasty; grandson of
Genghis Khan

Batu (bah-TOO)
Mongol leader of the
Golden Horde, which
controlled Russia;
grandson of Genghis
Khan

Timur (TEE-mer)
Central Asian
conqueror

CHAPTER SUMMARY

Although European, Chinese, and Muslim leaders generally looked down on the Mongols as violent nomads, no one could argue with their success. Unable to stand up to the strength of the Mongols, many rivals and enemies became allies. Although the Mongols were often merciless and brutal, they were tolerant of other religions, and treated submissive enemies less harshly than combative ones. By the middle of the 13th century, the Mongol grasp on Asia began to loosen, and in 1368, Ming forces in China overthrew the Mongols' Yuan Dynasty.

PERFORMANCE OBJECTIVES

▶ To understand how the Mongols built their empire

▶ To explain how the Mongols benefited international trade and culture

▶ To compare and contrast how Mongol allies, rivals, and enemies reacted to them

▶ To understand why and how Mongol control of Asia eventually weakened

BUILDING BACKGROUND

Review with students what they have already learned about the Mongols in Chapter 1. Then draw attention to the title and subtitle of Chapter 2. Ask students to make predictions regarding "who's next" on the Mongols' agenda of conquest, and what developments might have eventually led to the Mongols' reaching "their limit."

VOCABULARY

refugees people who flee their homes, due to war or other severe hardship

nomads people who travel from place to place

administrators managers of the daily operations of a business or government

allies countries, tribes, or groups joined together for a united purpose

rivals people or groups who compete against each other for the same prize

deception the act or practice of fooling someone with trickery

demise the downfall, end, or death

strategist a person who is very skilled in making complicated plans

As needed, have students consult the glossary to define the following words: *Assassins, heretical, infidel, Shi'a, steppe, victuals, yarlick.*

WORKING WITH PRIMARY SOURCES

Direct attention to the sidebar poem on Student Edition page 34 and ask a volunteer to read it aloud. Ask students to compare the "victory bulletins" mentioned in the poem to today's newspaper accounts of battles or wars.

GEOGRAPHY CONNECTION

Location Discuss the vast Mongol Empire of 1300 shown on Student Edition page 30. Guide students to use an atlas or world map to compare the size of the relatively small modern country of Mongolia. Discuss the geographic features that provided advantages for the Mongol Empire, and those that are advantages to Mongolia.

READING COMPREHENSION QUESTIONS

1. Why did such peoples as the English, Chinese, and Muslims have to rethink their negative views of the Mongols? (*Although the Mongols were violent and somewhat uncivilized, they were too successful to ignore or look down on.*)

2. Why did the Mongols want to conquer Korea? (*They wanted to take advantage of Korea's rice, soldiers, and navy—things that they lacked.*)

3. How did Chinese writers and artists protest the harsh rule of the Mongols? (*They wrote plays and created pieces of art that subtly criticized the Mongols.*)

4. What factors may have helped Europe and Japan to escape Mongol conquest? (*The Mongols may have found it difficult to wage wars in heavily wooded areas in Europe. Japan may have escaped due to storms that destroyed two Mongol invasion attempts.*)

5. Who was Timur? (*He was a Turkish Muslim who tried to exert his will in Asia in ways similar to those of Genghis Khan. He was brutal, and, unlike, Genghis Khan, had little religious tolerance. He eventually defeated the Golden Horde and the Ottomans, but he died before he could conquer China.*)

6. What finally caused the demise of the Mongol Empire? (*In 1368, Ming forces overthrew the Yuan Dynasty. To the west, quarrels between Mongol rulers weakened the empire.*)

CRITICAL THINKING QUESTIONS

1. In what ways did the Mongols' rivals follow the old proverb, "If you can't beat them, join them"? (*The Mongols were so powerful that many of their rivals chose to work with them rather than against them. Since the Mongols had no written language and no knowledge of government, they used Uighurs as administrators and record keepers.*)

2. Explain how both the Mongols and the Assassins used force and deception to fight and conquer their enemies. (*The Mongols promised the Assassins that they could join their forces, but then they killed their leaders and dismantled their forts. The Assassins sometimes put members of their group inside their enemies' households and then, on signal, killed everyone.*)

3. Why did the Mongols take a Chinese name, the Yuan Dynasty, for the portion of their empire in China? (*They needed administrators to control the local government. Therefore, they took a Chinese name, ordered that the records be kept in Chinese, and mixed Chinese traditions with Mongol customs.*)

SOCIAL SCIENCES

Civics Have students reread the final paragraph on Student Edition page 36. Discuss why the creation of stronger central governments might have been a shrewd strategy for making a nation less vulnerable to attack. Relate the discussion to the federal government of the United States.

THEN and NOW

After the death of Genghis Khan, his empire eventually broke apart, and the Mongols came under Chinese rule. The independent nation of Mongolia was established in 1921, but was controlled by the Soviet Union. Only now is modern Mongolia is ruled by an elected president, a prime minister, and a parliament.

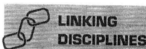

LINKING DISCIPLINES

Drama To show the subservience the Khubilai Khan demanded from his courtiers, have students act out the scene described by Marco Polo in the primary source on Student Edition page 28. Have one student play Marco Polo and read the excerpt as a narrator while other students pantomime the scene Polo describes.

READING AND LANGUAGE ARTS

Reading Nonfiction   As students read, have them use a three-column chart to compare and contrast Genghis Khan, Khubilai Khan, and Timur (Student Edition pages 28, 34, 36). Students might note details in categories such as *Leadership Style, Achievements,* and *Area Ruled.* This activity may be used to assess students' understanding of these Mongol leaders.

Using Language   The author uses several idioms in this chapter. Make sure that students understand the meanings of *up to* (page 27); *dogs* (page 27); *lumped them together* (page 29); *a slice of the tax collection money* (page 31); *pretty well* (page 33); *puppet* (page 34); and *rough and tumble world* (page 35).

WRITING

Persuasive Essay   Have students choose a point of view for dealing with the Mongols: (1) "If you can't beat them, join them"; (2) "Just wait them out"; or (3) "Life with the Mongols is better than this." Have each student write a persuasive essay to support the chosen point of view. Provide time for students to share and discuss their essays.

SUPPORTING LEARNING

English Language Learners   Work with students to find and discuss the meanings of words beginning with the prefix *re-,* meaning "again" (*rethinking, readjust, reintroducing,* and *replacing*); the prefix *un-,* meaning "not" (*unfamiliar, unbeatable,* and *unarmed*; and the suffix *–less,* meaning "without" (*homeless* and *merciless*). Encourage them to create sections in their notebooks for new words containing these word parts.

Struggling Readers   Before they begin reading Chapter 2, work with students to set up a "Who's Who" chart, with sections labeled *Genghis Khan, Khubilai Khan, Batu, Ogodei,* and *Timur* (Tamberlane). Based on the information in Chapter 1, have them jot down details regarding these men. Then, as they read Chapter 2, have them add further details to help them to keep track of "Who's Who" in the Mongol world.

EXTENDING LEARNING

Enrichment   Review the description of how the Chinese used their art to protest the rule of the Mongols on Student Edition page 32. Then ask students to research modern means of nonviolent protest. Students can begin their research by entering the words *nonviolent protest* in a search engine. Allow time for students to report their findings to the class.

Extension   Although the Mongols were often merciless conquerors, they also helped to foster and strengthen trade along the Silk Road. Have students work with partners or small groups to learn more about the Mongols' role in international commerce, as chronicled by Marco Polo and others.

THE MONGOL EMPIRE, 1300

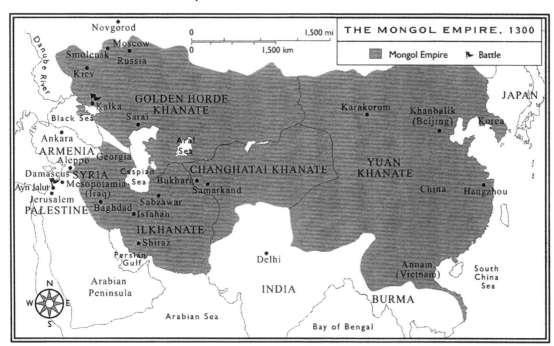

Directions

Use the map and your book to answer the questions that follow.

1. At its widest point, the Mongol Empire stretched from Kiev to Korea. Use the mileage scale to calculate about how many miles separate Kiev and Korea.

_____

_____

2. Which part of the Mongol Empire was controlled by Batu, the grandson of Genghis Khan? Circle its name on the map.

3. Which part of the Mongol Empire was controlled by Khubilai Khan, also a grandson of Genghis Khan? Underline its name on the map.

4. In 1300, which countries in Asia were not a part of the Mongol Empire?

_____

_____

5. What body of water in the western part of the Mongol Empire stands as a border between the Mongol Empire and other territories?

_____

_____

DINNER FIT FOR A KING

Directions

This excerpt from *The Travels of Marco Polo* appears on Student Edition page 28. In it, Marco Polo describes a scene at the court of Khubilai Khan. Read the passage and answer the questions that follow.

> In the middle of the hall, where the Great Khan sits at table, there is a magnificent piece of furniture, made in the form of a square coffer, each side of which is . . . exquisitely carved in figures of animals and gilt. It is hollow within for the purpose of receiving a capacious vase, of pure gold, calculated to hold many gallons. . . . The numerous persons who attend . . . his Majesty and serve him with victuals [food] and drink, are all obliged to cover their noses and mouths with handsome veils or cloths of worked silk, in order that his victuals or his wine may not be affected by their breath. When drink is called for by him, and the page in waiting presented it, he retires three paces and kneels down, upon which the courtiers, and all who are present, in like manner make their prostration. At the same moment all the musical instruments, of which theirs is a numerous band, begin to play and continue to do so until he has ceased drinking, when all the company recover their posture.

1. A coffer is a large box or chest. What do the coffer and its contents suggest about the wealth and luxuries surrounding Khubilai Khan? Explain.

_____

_____

_____

_____

2. What rules govern the people who serve Khubilai Khan his food and drink?

_____

_____

_____

3. Why might Khubilai Khan have made rules about what the court must do while he drinks his wine?

_____

_____

_____

4. What do you think Marco Polo thought of what he witnessed in Khubilai Khan's dining hall? Why do you think so?

_____

_____

_____

_____

A. COMPREHENSION

Circle the letter of the best answer for each question.

1. People who looked down on the Mongols as uncivilized nomads had to readjust their thinking because
   a. the Mongols sent the Assassins to force them to submit.
   b. the Mongols were extremely successful.
   c. the Mongols had no written language.
   d. the Mongols used a Chinese name for part of their empire.

2. Marco Polo visited the Chinese court of Khubilai Khan because
   a. Khubilai Khan asked him to become the Mongols' historian.
   b. he was a prisoner that the Mongols had captured in Korea.
   c. he was a Chinese artist who was told to decorate Khubilai Khan's palace.
   d. he was a prominent trader from Venice, doing business in China.

3. Which statement best describes the Mongols' strategies for conquest?
   a. They relied on naval power to conquer many territories.
   b. They relied on slow infantry marches rather than horses.
   c. They relied on force and deception to conquer many territories.
   d. They usually offered treasures to the rulers of lands they wished to conquer.

4. Which statement best describes how the Mongols treated the people they conquered?
   a. They killed only those people who had different religious views than they had.
   b. They killed city people, but saved farmers.
   c. They taxed the people heavily, but encouraged trade and offered religious tolerance.
   d. They forced the people to adopt the Mongol customs and written language.

B. SHORT ANSWER

Answer each question in two or three sentences.

5. What methods did Chinese writers and artists use to criticize the Mongols? Give one example.

_____

_____

_____

6. How did the Mongol Empire end?

_____

_____

_____

C. WRITING

On a separate sheet of paper, write an essay explaining how Timur and Genghis Khan were alike and different.

TWICE AS POWERFUL: POLAND AND LITHUANIA UNITE PAGES 37–47

CHAPTER 3

FOR HOMEWORK

STUDENT STUDY GUIDE

pages 19–22

CAST OF CHARACTERS

Jogaila (JOH-gai-luh) king of Poland and Lithuania, ruled with Jadwiga

Jadwiga (JAH-dwee-guh) queen of Poland, joint ruler with Jogaila

Vytautas (vih-TAO-tuhs) Grand Duke of Lithuania

Nicolaus Copernicus (kuh-PER-nih-khus) Polish astronomer

Jan Sobieski (SOH-bee-skee) king of Poland, saved Vienna from Turkish invasion

CHAPTER SUMMARY

Poland and Lithuania began to unite during the 14th century in order to protect themselves against common enemies. Royal marriages brought the two lands together and formed Europe's largest empire. During the Renaissance, the Polish astronomer Nicolaus Copernicus changed the way people viewed the universe. Over time, the Polish and Lithuanian Commonwealth weakened, and by 1800, the two countries had disappeared as independent nations.

PERFORMANCE OBJECTIVES

▸ To analyze Poland and Lithuania's geographic location and features

▸ To understand the impact of missing the plague on these countries

▸ To explain the significance of the work of Nicolaus Copernicus

▸ To describe the conflict between scientific advances and religious beliefs

BUILDING BACKGROUND

Begin a discussion about why countries might decide to become allies. Ask students what advantages an alliance might afford, such as mutual military support, the sharing of resources, or political, social, and economic goals. Explain that in Chapter 3 they will learn why Poland and Lithuania developed an alliance in the 14th century.

VOCABULARY

clan a group of relatives, friends, or associates

controversial not agreed upon; disputed

pagan follower of certain non-Christian beliefs or practices

heretics people who don't believe in accepted religious thought

modernizing making something up to date or current

partition the division of something into parts

As needed, have students consult the glossary to define the following words: *deluge, dominion, magnate, szlachta, veni, vidi, deus vinxit.*

WORKING WITH PRIMARY SOURCES

Point out the photograph of the trumpeter in Krakow on Student Edition page 37. Explain that a hymn, also known as the Krakow signal, is trumpeted hourly, and is broadcast at noon on Polish radio. Invite students to hear the Krakow signal at *www.krakow-info.com/hejnal.htm*. Discuss how the Krakow signal connects modern-day Polish people with their past.

GEOGRAPHY CONNECTION

Region Use a current map to compare the borders of present-day Poland and Lithuania with the map on Student Edition page 38. Discuss how the lack of natural geographic borders, such as mountains and rivers, might contribute to changing territories and power.

READING COMPREHENSION QUESTIONS

1. How did Poland and Lithuania view each other prior to the 1300s? Why did they begin to work toward an alliance? (*The two countries had religious differences, and had struggled for control of land and sea trade. They began to form an alliance during the 1300s against common enemies such as the Tartars and the Teutonic Knights.*)

2. How did royal marriages help unite Poland and Lithuania? (*Marriages between the royals of Poland and Lithuania helped form an empire, and as Lithuanians began to convert to Christianity, religion served to unify the people.*)

3. How did Jogaila and Vytautas defeat the Teutonic Knights at the Battle of Grunwald? (*They used Mongol strategies that allowed them to devastate the Teutonic Knights and their leaders.*)

4. How did the work of Nicolaus Copernicus change the way Europeans saw the universe? (*Copernicus determined that the sun, not the earth, was the center of the universe, which brought a profound shift in thinking.*)

5. What factors contributed to the decline called "the Deluge"? (*Wars on Polish land weakened the economy; magnates gained control of land, and neighboring countries took territory from the empire until the two countries were eventually taken over.*)

CRITICAL THINKING QUESTIONS

1. What was the effect of the plague on Poland and Lithuania? How did this appear as a threat to other groups in the region? (*Poland and Lithuania were not devastated by the plague, and others in the region felt threatened by these countries' growing population and power.*)

2. How was Copernicus able to pursue his work even though his book was later banned by Catholic leaders? (*Poland's policies of tolerance enabled Copernicus to follow his work.*)

3. How did the openness of the Polish and Lithuanian Commonwealth extend to the everyday lives of its people? (*Because they were elected, monarchs and officials were accountable to the people. Lithuanian women were also given legal equality.*)

SOCIAL SCIENCES

Civics Discuss the attributes of the democratic government in the Polish and Lithuanian Commonwealth. Encourage students to compare the role and power of its monarchy with constitutional monarchies and democracies with which they are familiar.

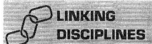

THEN and **NOW**

During early medieval times, Poland was primarily Christian and Lithuanians followed their own polytheistic religious beliefs. Today, most citizens of both countries identify themselves as Roman Catholics.

LINKING DISCIPLINES

Science The work of the 14th-century Muslim astronomer Ibn al-Shafir included heliocentric, or sun-centered, theories, and it is possible that his work may have influenced Copernicus. Encourage students to learn more about heliocentric theories and report their findings to the class.

READING AND LANGUAGE ARTS

Reading Nonfiction As a class, work together to compose questions that restate main ideas from the chapter, such as, *Why did Poland and Lithuania begin to see themselves as allies in the 1300s?* Then have students work independently to identify and list details that help answer each question.

Using Language Have students examine the descriptions of Jogaila, Jadwiga, their "courtship," and their marriage on Student Edition pages 40–41. Work together to make one list of descriptive details related to their personal lives and another list of details related to their political achievements. Discuss how the details enhance students' understanding of the historical figures.

WRITING

Explanation Have students write an essay that Nicolaus Copernicus might have written, explaining the general ideas of his advances in astronomy. Essays should also acknowledge the way that his work is likely to be viewed by the church, and why. Students' essays may used to assess their understanding of Copernicus's ideas.

SUPPORTING LEARNING

English Language Learners Guide students to develop lists of word families in their journals. Work together to scan the chapter for words such as *Christian, Christianity, non-Christian; allies, alliance, allied; and tolerance, tolerate, tolerant.* Have volunteers identify the prefixes and suffixes added to each root or base word, and explain how the word parts change the words' meanings or parts of speech.

Struggling Readers Encourage students to create an "allies and enemies" chart or diagram that shows how Poland and Lithuania came to work together, who they worked against and why, and other groups or countries they worked with to defeat common enemies. Have pairs of students share and discuss their work.

EXTENDING LEARNING

Enrichment Like Leonardo da Vinci, Nicolaus Copernicus was a true "Renaissance man." Invite students to use library and electronic resources to learn more about this multi-talented man and create a classroom display that tells about his many interests, achievements, and accomplishments.

Extension Have small groups of students write and perform scenes that enact various parts of the Battle of Grunwald. For example, one scene might present the events leading up to the battle, and others might describe battle events or discussions about strategies.

NAME _____ **DATE** _____

POLAND AND LITHUANIA, 1500–1582

Directions

Use the map to answer the questions that follow.

1. Had the lands of Poland and Lithuania increased or decreased by 1582?

_____

2. What new land did the Polish and Lithuanian Commonwealth include by 1582?

_____

_____

3. Which cities were a part of the Jagiellon dominions in 1500 but were not a part of the Polish and Lithuanian Commonwealth by 1582?

_____

_____

4. About how far was the Battle of Tannenberg from the city of Warsaw?

_____

5. How did Poland and Lithuania control sea trade between 1500 and 1582?

_____

_____

6. What advantage might Baltic Sea trade bring to the Polish and Lithuanian Commonwealth?

_____

_____

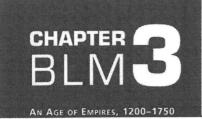

VOTE EARLY AND ARMORED

Directions

This excerpt describes the election of a Polish king, probably in 1648. It is from a book written by a French engineer in 1744. The passage also appears on Student Edition page 44. Read the excerpt, and answer the questions that follow.

[The election of the king] is generally held in [an] open field half a league from Warsaw . . . [in a] small inclosure . . . about 1000 or 1200 paces in compass, enclosed by a pitiful ditch about five or six foot wide, which serves only to hinder horses from going into the said inclosure; [inside] there are two great tents, one for the election where all the Senators sit and the other where all the Deputies of Provinces met who confer together before they go into the Great Audience of the Senate. . . . They meet thus every day . . . , during time they pose all they can think on toward preserving their liberties . . . During the election of the late King Valdislaws, there were no less than 80,000 horses about that little inclosure, all soldiers following the Senators, for every one of them had a little army. . . . Everyone is attended by his friends and subjects . . . with a resolution to fight in case they cannot agree. Observe, that all the nobility of the country was upon its guard, every one with his foot in the stirrup ready to mount upon the least disagreement of falling out, to fall on those that should attempt to infringe their liberties. At length, after several sittings and audiences, they agreed upon a Prince for their King; every one or at least the chief of the Senators and Deputies, put his hand to it. . . . Then everyone, returning to Quarters, gives orders to his troops to be ready to draw up according to the Great General's command, under the great Standard [flag] of the Crown and were ready to cry, "Long live the King" calling him by his name. . . . Next day they conducted him to St. John's Church at Warsaw where before the Altar the King took his Oath.

1. Why did each of the Senators have "a little army" present? Why was it important that the new king had the support of these "armies"?

_____

_____

2. How would the next king be elected if the Senators and Deputies could not come to an agreement?

_____

_____

3. Why do you think "preserving liberties" was so important?

_____

_____

4. Why do you think these elections were held in a public place with so many people present?

_____

_____

5. How did Poland's election of a ruler differ from the way other countries passed power from one monarch to another? Which system seems better to you?

_____

_____

A. COMPREHENSION

Circle the letter of the best answer to each question.

1. The primary reason Poland and Lithuania decided to unite was
   a. because Poland had been weakened by battles with Lithuania.
   b. because their shared religious beliefs made them a powerful force.
   c. to defend themselves against common enemies.
   d. to strengthen their democratic governments.

2. Polish and Lithuanian leaders were
   a. chosen by the Pope.
   b. members of the royal classes whose power was passed on through inheritance.
   c. appointed by the military leaders of the Commonwealth.
   d. elected by the gentry and city leaders.

3. One factor that contributed to Poland and Lithuania's strength was
   a. that since they had not been affected by the plague, their populations grew.
   b. their decision to allow each country to follow its own religions.
   c. their clear geographic borders of mountains and seas.
   d. that they had peacefully shared control of Baltic trade for centuries.

4. The work of Copernicus showed that
   a. he was only interested in astrology.
   b. the sun, not the earth, was the center of the solar system.
   c. church leaders accepted new ideas of man's place in the universe.
   d. the sun and other planets revolved around the earth.

5. During the time referred to as "the Deluge,"
   a. the Polish and Lithuanian Commonwealth was nearly destroyed by floods.
   b. Poland and Lithuania combined forces to establish an empire.
   c. the Polish and Lithuanian Commonwealth was weakened by setbacks.
   d. Poland and Lithuania defeated the Teutonic Knights and claimed their lands.

B. SHORT ANSWER

Explain each topic.

6. Poland's religious beliefs: _____

_____

7. Lithuania's religious beliefs: _____

_____

8. The role of religion in the marriage of Jogaila and Jadwiga: _____

_____

9. Make a generalization about the impact of this marriage on Lithuanians. _____

_____

_____

_____

_____

CHAPTER 4

TROUBLED TIMES, TROUBLED TSARS: THE RUSSIAN EMPIRE
PAGES 48–59

CAST OF CHARACTERS

Ivan the Terrible tsar who defeated Tartars and extended Russia into Siberia

Alexis tsar who began westernization

Sophia ruled Russia for her brothers, continued westernization of the country

Peter the Great tsar who founded St. Petersburg

CHAPTER SUMMARY

The Russians unified under the leadership of the city of Moscow. Ivan the Terrible ruled with the help of the special police and used the military to expand the empire. After his death, the Romanovs began a royal dynasty. Alexis, Sophia, and Peter the Great began to modernize Russia. They punished or exiled those who rebelled against the change. Peter moved the capital from Moscow to a new city on the Baltic Sea, named St. Petersburg.

PERFORMANCE OBJECTIVES

▶ To analyze political change in the Russian Empire in the 16th, 17th, and 18th centuries

▶ To examine economic change in the Russian Empire in the 16th, 17th, and 18th centuries

BUILDING BACKGROUND

Write the names *Ivan the Terrible* and *Peter the Great* on the board and explain that they were rulers of the Russian Empire. Have students preview the chapter and speculate why each person got his nickname. Tell them that they will read about these leaders' influence on Russian history, and that both men had good and bad aspects to their rule.

VOCABULARY

steppe large, flat treeless areas of land in southeastern Europe or Asia

tsar Russian ruler

boyars Russian nobles

oprichniki a special secret police that Ivan the Terrible established in Russia

strelsty musketeers of the Russian army

terem a secluded part of a home where upper-class Russian women stayed

As needed, have students consult the glossary to define the following words: *Domonstroia, icon.*

WORKING WITH PRIMARY SOURCES

Direct students' attention to the letter about Peter the Great on Student Edition page 56. Discuss the historical context of the letter and why historians might want additional information to verify the author's account. Where could they find information to verify Peter the Great's trip? Invite interested students to learn more about Peter the Great at *www.bartleby.com/65/pe/Peter1-Rus.html.*

GEOGRAPHY CONNECTION

Interaction As students read about the Russian Empire, have them use a world map to locate the nations of people who influenced Russia, such as the Dutch builders of St. Petersburg.

READING COMPREHENSION QUESTIONS

1. Who were the two primary enemies of the Russians? (*the Mongols and the Tartars*)
2. What happened to thousands of captured Russians and Ukrainians? (*They were sold into slavery in the Middle East.*)
3. What was a military achievement of Ivan the Terrible? (*He pushed back the Tartars from the Russian cities of Kazan and Astrakhan and opened up Siberia.*)
4. How did the Romanovs modernize their army? (*They recruited foreign officers to train soldiers in new techniques.*)
5. What was Russian education like before the Romanovs? (*There were no universities and no formal schools except for those training the Orthodox clergy.*)

CRITICAL THINKING QUESTIONS

1. Why was Moscow priest Filipp brave to confront Ivan the Terrible about the oprichniki? (*The oprichniki* brutally punished or killed Ivan the Terrible's enemies. When Filipp spoke up against the injustice and violence, he risked provoking Ivan's anger. He was killed.)
2. Why might it have been a political risk for the Romanovs to bring foreign officers into the Russian army, and to introduce new ideas socially? (*The local population was suspicious of foreigners, as well as new ideas; they might have rebelled.*)
3. How did Western ideas affect Peter's views of Russia's military and society? (*He used what he learned in Holland and England to modernize the navy. He gave women more rights in marriage and to control their property.*)
4. How did Peter's daughter Elizabeth modernize with more tolerance than her father? Give an example. (*Possible answer: Peter put down a revolt with torture, public executions, and the imprisonment of Sophia. Elizabeth tried to outlaw the death penalty and the torture of people under seventeen.*)

SOCIAL SCIENCES

Science, Technology, and Society Have interested students learn more about the technology used to build the city of St. Petersburg. They can present what they learned in a panel discussion. One useful website is *www.saint-petersburg.com/history/foundation.asp.*

Reading Nonfiction The chapter discusses the rule of Ivan the Terrible and Peter the Great. Suggest that students create problem-solution charts for each ruler. They can meet to discuss what influenced each ruler to make those decisions.

Using Language Have students investigate the etymology of the vocabulary terms. Suggest that they categorize them as Russian-based words that are part of the English language or Russian (foreign) terms. Point out that the foreign terms are italicized in their textbooks.

WRITING

Write a Summary Instruct students to write a summary of the chapter. Remind them to include the main ideas and the most significant details, and to use their own words. Suggest they read aloud their drafts with a partner before revising them. Use the summaries to assess students' understanding of chapter content.

SUPPORTING LEARNING

English Language Learners Draw students' attention to the adverbial clause *For seven years* in the sentence *For seven years, the oprichniki swept into people's homes* . . . on Student Edition page 51. Explain that like adverbs, adverbial clauses tell *how, why, when,* or *where.* Invite students to find other examples of adverbial clauses and explain which of the questions they answer.

Struggling Readers Work with students to find examples of how the tsars' exposure to new ideas led to reforms in the Russian Empire. Suggest that they create before-and-after charts and share them with a partner.

EXTENDING LEARNING

Enrichment Have students research the history and geography of Siberia and write journal entries from the point of view of a settler in the 1600s. They can use details from the chapter, as well as websites such as *www.infoplease.com/ce6/world/A0861075.html.*

Extension Suggest that students learn more about the cultural hierarchy in the Russian Empire. Have them make a pyramid diagram to identify the social classes.

PRAISING ST. PETERSBURG

Directions

Excerpt A, comparing Moscow and St. Petersburg, is by Russian poet Alexander Pushkin. It also appears on Student Edition page 54. Excerpt B is by a German visitor to St. Petersburg named Friedrich Weber, written in 1714. It also appears on Student Edition page 58. Read the excerpts, and answer the questions that follow.

Excerpt A: Old Moscow's paled before this other metropolis [St. Petersburg]: it's just the same as when a widowed Empress Mother bows to a young Tsaritsa's* claim.
* wife or widow of a tsar

Excerpt B: When I arrived there, I was expected to find . . . a heap of villages linked together like a plantation in the West Indies . . . however, St. Petersburg may with reason be looked upon as a wonder of the world considering its palaces, sixty-odd thousand houses and the short time that was employed in the building of it.

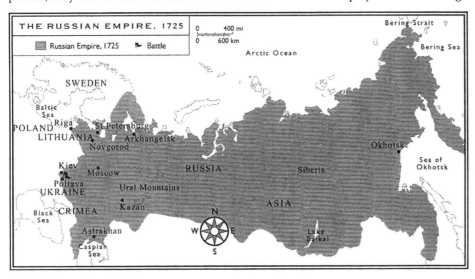

1. How does Excerpt A compare St. Petersburg to Moscow? _____

_____

2. How does Excerpt B compare St. Petersburg to a West Indies plantation? _____

_____

3. How are the two opinions about St. Petersburg similar? _____

_____

4. What information in Excerpt B could be verified? _____

_____

5. Why might later governments have moved Russia's capital back to Moscow? _____

_____

TALL, DARK, AND HANDSOME

Directions

This excerpt is from a letter about Peter the Great by Sophia, electress of Hanover. Written in 1687, it also appears on Student Edition page 56. Read the excerpt, and answer the questions that follow.

> The Tsar is very tall, his features are fine, and his figure very noble. He has a great vivacity of mind, and a ready and just repartee. But, with all the advantages with which nature has endowed him, it could be wished that his manners were a little less rustic [coarse, untrained]. . . . We stayed in truth a very long time at table, but we would gladly have remained there longer still without feeling a moment of boredom, for the Tsar was in a very good humor and never ceased talking to us. My daughters had her Italians sing. Their song pleased him though he confessed to us that he did not care much for music.
>
> I asked him if he liked hunting. He replied that his father had been very fond of it, but that he himself, from his earliest youth, had a real passion for navigation and fireworks. He told us that he worked himself in building ships, showed us his hands, and made us touch the callous places that had been caused by work.

1. What do you think Peter the Great was like, based on this letter?

_____

_____

_____

2. What criticism does the author have toward Peter the Great?

_____

_____

_____

3. Based on what you learned in the chapter, why do you think he was interested in building ships?

_____

_____

_____

4. What do you think "a ready and just repartee" means? Use a dictionary to help you.

_____

_____

_____

5. List three questions about Sophia's letter that could be answered by historical research.

_____

_____

_____

6. How might Peter's enjoyment of his evening with Sophia and her daughter have fit into his later ending of "terems"?

_____

_____

_____

A. COMPREHENSION

Circle the letter of the best answer for each question.

1. Why were the Tartars able to defeat the Russians?
   a. They offered to treat the Russians fairly if they would surrender.
   b. They had the use of gunpowder, and the Russians did not.
   c. They used multiple horses for quick, long-range attacks.
   d. They had a stronger, more modern navy.

2. Which city's leaders unified Russia against the Mongols and the Tartars?
   a. Moscow   c. St. Petersburg
   b. Kazan   d. Riga

3. What was the main reason why Ivan IV established a secret police?
   a. to punish the *strelsty* after they rioted   c. to punish his perceived enemies
   b. to persecute non-Christians   d. to persecute foreign immigrants

4. Which of the following was not one of Peter the Great's reforms?
   a. modernizing the navy
   b. outlawing torture
   c. giving more rights to women
   d. having men attend secular schools

5. How did Peter's daughter Elizabeth continue the Westernization of Russia?
   a. She was the first to send Russian nobles to be educated in Europe.
   b. She convinced the Old Believers to support her ideas.
   c. She built St. Petersburg in honor of her father.
   d. She financed great architecture, such as the Winter Palace.

B. SHORT ANSWER

Write two or three sentences to answer each question.

6. Why might "terrified" be a better word than "terrible" to describe Ivan IV?

_____

_____

_____

7. For what reasons might Russia not have built up its navy before the time of Peter the Great?

_____

_____

_____

C. COMPARE AND CONTRAST

On a separate sheet of paper, write an essay in which you compare and contrast the reigns of Ivan the Terrible and Peter the Great.

CHAPTER 5

THE REAL MUGHALS, NOT THE REEL MOGULS: EMPIRE IN INDIA
PAGES 60–71

FOR HOMEWORK

STUDENT STUDY GUIDE

pages 27–30

CHAPTER SUMMARY

The Mughal Empire was founded by Babur, a Turkish Muslim and descendant of the Mongols. In the 16th and 17th centuries, a series of Mughal emperors, including Akbar, Shah Jahan, and Aurangzeb, ruled India. At its peak, the Mughal Empire encouraged trade and created beautiful art and architecture. Although the Mughals were Muslims, most of them were religiously tolerant.

PERFORMANCE OBJECTIVES

▶ To identify the leaders of the Mughal Empire

▶ To understand the Mughals' accomplishments and conflicts

▶ To understand how the Mughals encouraged the cultural blending of religions and granted some rights to women

BUILDING BACKGROUND

Write the word *façade* on the chalkboard, and ask a volunteer to find its definition in the dictionary. If necessary, explain that the set for a movie or play often includes façades that give the appearance of entire buildings. Explain that students will read about an empire whose leaders gave the appearance of great wealth while most of their people lived in terrible poverty. Discuss the problems that might arise from this situation.

CAST OF CHARACTERS

Akbar (AHK-bahr) Mughal emperor who ruled 1556–1605, at height of empire

Aurangzeb (oh-rahng-ZEHB) last of the major Mughal rulers

Babur ("The Tiger") (BAH-ber) founder of the Mughal Empire

VOCABULARY

pomp a display of wealth or magnificence

tyrant an absolute ruler who rules in an overly harsh way

rebellions actions taken against one's government

sultanate the land or government ruled by a sultan

artillery heavy, mounted guns, including cannon

sovereigns rulers such as kings, queens, or emperors

diplomacy actions that a government takes to maintain peaceful relationships with other nations

As needed, have students consult the glossary to define the following words: *harem, jizya.*

WORKING WITH PRIMARY SOURCES

Read the sidebar on Student Edition page 63, and talk about the problems the speaker cites. Ask students which parts of the statement seem realistic, and which may be exaggerations. Discuss what the leader of the Hindu Maratha resistance might have hoped to gain by making the statement.

GEOGRAPHY CONNECTION

Region Use a modern map of India from an atlas or an online source to compare and contrast the modern nation with the territory of the Mughal Empire, shown on the map on Student Edition page 61. Point out that at its peak, the Mughal Empire covered all but the most southern tip of India, as well as parts of Pakistan, Kashmir, and Afghanistan.

READING COMPREHENSION QUESTIONS

1. How did the Mughal Empire get its name? (*They were at least partly descended from the Mongols.*)

2. What was Babur's role in the Mughal Empire? (*Babur was the founder of the empire and its first emperor.*)

3. Why were there so many fierce fights and rivalries within the families of the emperors? (*The eldest son of the emperor did not automatically inherit the throne. Therefore, sons and brothers all fought with each other to become the next emperor.*)

4. What were Akbar's accomplishments? (*Under his leadership, the empire expanded greatly, through both wars and diplomacy. A Muslim, he was religiously tolerant, and attempted to create a new, inclusive religion. Also during his rule, art and architecture thrived.*)

5. What is the Taj Mahal, and why was it built? (*It is a huge and glorious marble structure, in Agra, which Shah Jahan built as a tomb for his wife.*)

CRITICAL THINKING QUESTIONS

1. What details support the idea that Babur was both a dedicated warrior and a sensitive, wise man? (*He repeatedly led an army against his rivals, and ultimately succeeding in defeating them, to found the empire. He was also very loyal and generous to his soldiers and an eloquent speaker and writer.*)

2. Why do you think that no major universities were founded during the Mughal Empire? (*Emperors may have been more focused on wealth than on learning, and were not university educated themselves. With so much poverty in the empire, people had to focus on surviving rather than on education.*)

4. How did Akbar's policy of religious tolerance benefit the Mughal Empire? (*People of Muslim, Hindu, Sikh, and Christian faiths could live together peacefully. The elimination of the jizya tax probably helped non-Muslims to live more comfortably. The building of Hindu and Sikh temples probably provided jobs.*)

SOCIAL SCIENCES

Economics Have students reread the final paragraph on Student Edition page 64, regarding the system of land taxes that Akbar developed. Discuss why this was a fair system, based on what the land could produce. Compare this system to the United States's system of graduated income tax.

THEN and NOW

While Mughal emperors enjoyed lavish wealth, most of the population lived in poverty. Modern India is still plagued with poverty; 25 percent of the population lives below the poverty level. However, many highly educated people in India enjoy successful careers in India's movie and technology industries.

LINKING DISCIPLINES

Architecture So many grand buildings were built during Akbar's reign that a style of architecture has been termed "Akbari." Students may enjoy taking a virtual tour of Mughal palaces and gardens, at *www.mughalgardens.org.* Have students investigate and report on the buildings' designs.

**LITERATURE
CONNECTION**

There are numerous enjoyable books that will broaden students' knowledge of the Mughal Empire.

Ganeri, Anita. *India Under the Mughal Empire, 1526–1858.* Raintree Publishing, 1998. Nonfiction. This book surveys the reigns of the six greatest Mughal emperors. EASY

Hambly, Gavin R. G. *Babur's Women: Elite Women in Late Medieval Central Asia and North India.* Palgrave Macmillan, 2005. Nonfiction. Based on Babur's memoirs, the author describes the involvement of women in the court and in camps. AVERAGE

Mukherji, Anisha Shekhar. *The Red Fort of Shahjahanabad.* Oxford University Press, 2003. Nonfiction. The architecture and history of the Red Fort of Delhi are studied in this book. AVERAGE

LITERACY TIPS

In addition to using the suggestions in the Supporting Learning and Extending Learning sections, refer back frequently to pages 16–19 for strategies and advice from a literacy coach.

READING AND LANGUAGE ARTS

Reading Nonfiction   Have students create a three-column chart with the headings *Ruler, Relationship,* and *Accomplishments.* As students read, have them list each Mughal ruler's name, his relationship to Babur, and his accomplishments. This activity may be used to assess students' understanding of chapter content.

Using Language   Discuss how the meanings of smaller words blend to create new meanings in a compound word. Challenge students to find examples of compound words as they read and discuss the meaning of each one. Examples include *present-day, snowstorm, grandmother, throughout* (page 63); *elsewhere* (page 65); *childbirth* (page 67); *non-Muslims, outlawed* (page 68); *well educated, battle-trained* (page 70).

WRITING

Journal Entry   Have students write journal entries describing a visit to the Taj Mahal. Tell them to include a description of the building, something about the building's history, and their impressions of the structure.

SUPPORTING LEARNING

English Language Learners   In their notebooks, have students create a Synonyms Chart, as shown below. Guide them to use a dictionary and a thesaurus to find simple synonyms for such words as injustice, instability (page 61) and rapt, fierce (page 62.)

Page	Word	Synonym
60	lavish	fancy, rich
60	absolute	total
60	reigned	ruled, led

Struggling Readers   Have students work with a partner to list details that describe a Mughal ruler. The details might refer to the leader's personality, or to his accomplishments. Tell partners to write each detail on a separate index card, without the leader's name. Collect the cards, shuffle them, and read each detail aloud. Challenge students to name the ruler the detail describes.

EXTENDING LEARNING

Enrichment   Invite students to write and perform skits that focus on the Mughal emperors. Have them scan the chapter for situations and quotations that illustrate the leaders' personalities, and then write scenes in which those characteristics are displayed. For example, students might perform a scene featuring Babur's refusal to seek shelter, as described on Student Edition page 63.

Extension   Under the Muslim rule of India, international trade flourished, standard weights and measurements were established, and such Indian products as calico and madras became popular in foreign lands. Suggest that students find out more about India's products and trade relationships with other countries during the era of the Mughals.

NAME   **DATE**

THE MUGHAL EMPIRE, 1530–1707

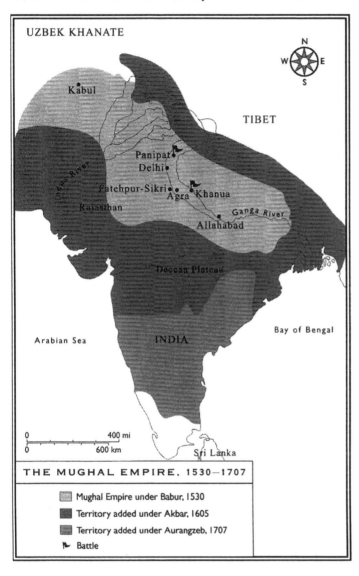

UZBEK KHANATE

Kabul

TIBET

Panipat
Delhi

Fatehpur-Sikri   Agra   Khanua

Rajasthan

Ganga River

Allahabad

Deccan Plateau

Arabian Sea

INDIA

Bay of Bengal

| 0 | | 400 mi |
| 0 | | 600 km |

Sri Lanka

THE MUGHAL EMPIRE, 1530—1707

▨ Mughal Empire under Babur, 1530
▨ Territory added under Akbar, 1605
▨ Territory added under Aurangzeb, 1707
⚑ Battle

Directions

Use the map to answer the questions that follow.

1. Which Mughal emperor was ruling when the empire reached its largest size?

_____

_____

_____

_____

_____

2. Why do you think most Mughal cities shown on the map are near rivers?

_____

_____

_____

_____

_____

3. Why do you think Akbar extended the empire to the Arabian Sea and the Bay of Bengal?

_____

_____

_____

_____

_____

_____

4. According to this map, what was the northernmost city in the Mughal Empire?

_____

_____

5. Describe the route that a traveler from Allahabad might take to visit the Taj Mahal in Agra.

_____

_____

WHISTLE WHILE YOU WORK

Directions

The following poem is from *The Medieval & Early Modern World Primary Sources and Reference Volume*, pages 61–62. It was written by an Indian woman between the 12th and 14th centuries. Read the poem and answer the questions that follow.

My spinning wheel is dear to me, my sister;
My household depends on it.
My husband married me and departed;
He went abroad to earn a living.

After twelve years he returned,
With a copper coin and a half;
He went to bathe in the Ganga,
Dropped the copper coin and a half.

Mother, father, father-in-law, mother-in-law,
One and all rejected us;
The spinning wheel was our savior,
To it we clung.

I paid off all my husband's debts
And over and above
Tying coin after coin in the corner of my sari
I earned a whole rupee.

1. "The Ganga" is the Ganges River. With that in mind, what events does the poem describe? Look up any unfamiliar words in a dictionary.

_____

_____

_____

2. What is the most probable reason that the woman's family rejected her and her husband?

_____

_____

_____

3. How did she repay her husband's debts?

_____

_____

_____

4. Why does the poet say that her spinning wheel is dear to her?

_____

_____

_____

5. How does the message in this poem relate to the freedoms and rights the Mughals afforded women?

_____

_____

_____

NAME   **DATE**

A. COMPREHENSION

Circle the letter of the best answer for each question.

1. The Mughal Empire was founded in 1494 by
   - **a.** Genghis Khan.
   - **b.** Akbar.
   - **c.** Babur.
   - **d.** Aurangzeb.

2. Akbar is considered the most gifted of the Mughal emperors because
   - **a.** he refused to take refuge during a battle, staying with his men instead.
   - **b.** he read many books and became a poet as well as an emperor.
   - **c.** he was a Hindu prince who converted to Islam and built many temples.
   - **d.** he was tolerant of many religions, promoted justice, and encouraged the arts.

3. The Taj Mahal was created as
   - **a.** a tomb for the emperor Shah Jahan's beloved wife.
   - **b.** a library for Akbar's vast collection of books.
   - **c.** a fort on the Ganges River.
   - **d.** a prison to which Aurangzeb sent even his own father and sister.

4. Which statement best describes the achievements of the Mughal emperors?
   - **a.** They built stately art museums and supported public education.
   - **b.** They converted a territory of open pastures into rich agricultural lands.
   - **c.** They used their wealth to build some of the world's most beautiful buildings.
   - **d.** They created lasting laws that guaranteed religious freedom.

B. SHORT ANSWER

Write two or three sentences to answer each question.

5. Why was Akbar's system of land taxes an example of his fairness?

_____

_____

_____

6. What was probably the most important reason that Mughal women were successful in business and in politics?

_____

_____

_____

C. WRITING

On Student Edition page 71, Akbar is quoted as saying, "we must not reject a thing that has been adopted by the wise men of other nations merely because we cannot find it in our book, or how shall we progress?" Based on what you've learned about him, does his statement make you think he was a wise leader, or was he an opportunist who wanted to take advantage of other nations? On a separate sheet of paper, write an essay to give your opinion, along with reasons to support it.

TRIUMPH OF THE TURKS: THE RISE OF THE OTTOMAN EMPIRE PAGES 72–82

CAST OF CHARACTERS

Beyazit (bay-AH-zeet), **"the Thunderbolt"** established Ottoman foothold in Europe

Timur (TEE-mer) Central Asian conqueror

Mehmet (meh-MEHT) **II, "the Conqueror"** Ottoman sultan who conquered Constantinople

CHAPTER SUMMARY

The Ottoman Turks came from the steppes of Central Asia to form an empire that eventually included Asia Minor, much of the Balkans, and the Middle East. The empire was unified around 1300 and lasted until 1923. Its military relied on enslaved Christian soldiers called Janissaries. The court officials and court women were enslaved as well. The official religion was Islam, but the Ottomans tolerated Christians and Jews. The Ottomans' greatest triumph was capturing Constantinople in 1453.

PERFORMANCE OBJECTIVES

▶ To explain the expansion of the Muslim rule through military conquests

▶ To analyze the cultural blending within Muslim civilizations

BUILDING BACKGROUND

Direct attention to the map of Constantinople on Student Edition page 72. Suggest that students use what they know about military campaigns to predict ways the Ottoman Turks might try to capture the city. Tell them that they will read about the battle and the expansion of the Ottoman Empire in this chapter.

VOCABULARY

sultan ruler

harem a separate, hidden part of a house for Muslim women

Valide Sultan mother of the sultan, or ruler, an important position

devsirme a gathering of Christian children every seven years by the Turks

Ulema the leaders of the Islamic court system within the Ottoman Empire

dhimmis people of the book; Ottoman name for Jews and Christians

WORKING WITH PRIMARY SOURCES

Have students discuss the lyric from a Christian song in the sidebar on Student Edition page 75. Discuss who the Janissaries were, and invite volunteers to explain the Janissaries' role in the Ottoman Empire. Elicit how the Christian point of view of Janissaries contrasted with that of the Ottoman Turks.

GEOGRAPHY CONNECTION

Movement Have students identify the location of Constantinople on the map on Student Edition page 75, and hypothesize about the movement of goods in and of the city through sea routes.

READING COMPREHENSION QUESTIONS

1. Where was the Ottoman's homeland? *(the steppes of Central Asia)*
2. What areas did the Ottoman Empire eventually control? *(Asia Minor, much of the Balkans, and the Middle East)*
3. Once they were part of the empire, why did the Serbians not want to fight for the Ottomans? *(They had been bitter enemies and Serbs were primarily Christian.)*
4. What was the significance of the Battle of Nicopolis, in what is now Bulgaria? *(The Ottomans defeated an alliance of European armies, killed 10,000 prisoners, and proved that they could expand in Europe.)*
5. How did the Ottomans treat Christians and Jews within their empire? *(They tolerated their religious beliefs, but non-Muslims had to pay a tax.)*

CRITICAL THINKING QUESTIONS

1. How did the rule of succession in the Ottoman leadership lead to conflicts? *(The sultans' sons fought each other to the death to become the new ruler.)*
2. How did certain enslaved women gain power during the "reign of women" from 1566 to 1666? *(The sultans did not marry, so they had children with Christian or Jewish slaves. As the mothers of potential sultans, these women had access to power.)*
3. What limited power did the Janissaries have? Explain. *(Possible answer: They had little power because they were slaves. They could, however, threaten to revolt, which was problematic because they were an elite military force.)*
4. How did new weaponry play a role in the defeat of Constantinople? *(The Ottomans had access to a powerful cannon, which was used to weaken the city's walls.)*

SOCIAL SCIENCES

Civics Suggest that pairs of students make a chart comparing the checks and balances between the sultans and the Ulema and checks and balances among the executive, legislative, and judicial branches of the United States government. Have the partners prepare an oral report to describe the similarities and differences they find.

READING AND LANGUAGE ARTS

Reading Nonfiction The chapter presents strong opinions from the author and from primary sources about the Ottomans. To track students' ability with this skill, have them distinguish between facts and opinions in several sample paragraphs.

Using Language Suggest that students create word webs for one or more leaders they read about in the chapter. Direct them to include adjectives or descriptive phrases and information that support those descriptions. This activity may be used to assess students' understanding of chapter content.

WRITING

Write a Narrative Review the leader of Byzantium's final speech to his people on Student Edition page 80. Remind students that Constantine XI knew it was a losing cause, but he had to prepare his people for battle. Have students write a narrative from the point of view of Constantine XI as he evaluates what has happened to his city and prepares to write the speech.

THEN and NOW

Istanbul, formerly Constantinople, straddles Europe and Asia. The old part of the city is on the European side and is still surrounded by parts of an ancient wall. Archaeologists continue to find remnants of the past. In 1998, they excavated the Great Palace of the Byzantine Empire.

LINKING DISCIPLINES

Art Have students study the architecture of the Hagia Sophia—both its Christian and Islamic influences. Instruct them to present a report on what they learned. Encourage them to make a cross-section diagram of the main dome. One useful site is *www.bartleby.com/65/ha/HagiaSop.html.*

There are numerous
enjoyable books that
will broaden students'
knowledge of the rise
of the Ottoman
Empire.

Goodwin, Godfrey. *The
Janissaries*. Saqi
Books, 1997.
Nonfiction. The history
of the Janissaries
shows times of victory
and of defeat.
AVERAGE

Inalcik, Halil. *The
Ottoman Empire: The
Classical Age
1300–1600*. Phoenix
Press, 2001.
Nonfiction. The author
presents the rise of
the Ottoman Empire
from a military power
to the most powerful
Islamic state of its
time. ADVANCED

McNeese, Tim.
Constantinople.
Chelsea House,
2003. Nonfiction. The
events surrounding
the 1453 siege of
Constantinople by
Turkish Muslims are
examined. EASY

LITERACY TIPS

In addition to using
the suggestions in the
Supporting Learning
and Extending
Learning sections,
refer back frequently
to pages 16–19 for
strategies and advice
from a literacy coach.

SUPPORTING LEARNING

English Language Learners Work with students to understand the syntax
of complex sentences. Help them rephrase and simplify sentences by identifying
who or *what* the sentence is about (the subject) and *what happened* (the verb).

Struggling Readers Direct students to complete a sequence of events chart
(see reproducibles at the back of this guide) to show each of the major battles
discussed in the chapter. Help them infer that with each victory, the Ottoman
Empire became stronger.

EXTENDING LEARNING

Enrichment Invite students to learn more about how the Ottomans
transformed Constantinople into an Islamic city. One useful Web site is
http://www.turizm.net/cities/istanbul/ottoman.html. They can present what they learn
in a bulletin board display with maps and photographs.

Extension Have small groups of students prepare and present a debate
between Ottoman supporters of the *devsirme* and Christian opponents. Remind
them to include facts from the chapter to support their arguments.

NAME _____ **DATE** _____

THE OTTOMAN EMPIRE, 1453

Directions
Use the map and the information in the chapter to answer the questions that follow.

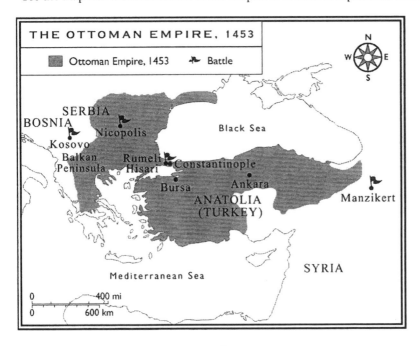

1. What three battles took place on the Balkan Peninsula?

_____

2. Which two battles took place within the Ottoman Empire?

_____

_____

_____

3. What was the shortest distance soldiers might have traveled between Kosovo and Nicopolis?

_____

_____

4. Why do you think the Ottomans wanted to control the southern coastline of Anatolia?

_____

_____

_____

5. What made Bursa a good meeting places for traders going by sea?

_____

_____

NAME _____   DATE _____

THE SULTANA'S LAST WISHES

Directions

This excerpt is from a book written by Evliya Celebi in the 17th century. It also appears on Student Edition page 81. The excerpt describes the will of a sultana named Kaya Sultan—the daughter of a sultan. The sultana prepared her will after she had a dream that foreshadowed her death. Read the excerpt, and answer the questions that follow.

> The pasha tried to console her in every way possible, but it was no use. The sultana grew more pious day by day. She gave 20,000 gold pieces in trust for Mecca and Medina*, and another 20,000 for the benefit of everyone in her household, great and small, including those off campaigning, the cooks, the [painters] and butlers, the falconers and her private staff. She provided in her will that 40,000 prayers be offered up for her soul nightly, stipulating 20,000 gold pieces to her trustee [for this purpose]. She also made provision for her own household retainers. . . . She gave over the deeds of her seventy gardens and vineyards, her summer palaces and estates—in short all of her real property—to her children and Melek's servants, with provision in her will that if the lineage came to an end, all revenue from her properties should go to the Holy Cities. For among the Sultanas of that period, none was wealthier than she. . . .
>
> It is a fact that, of the seventeen sultanas [daughters of the sultan] who were alive in those days, none got on with her husband so well as Kaya with Melek. She was, too, very clever and prudent in managing her household. She was a true daughter of Sultan Murad IV, a raging lioness, and a benefactress to all the other sultanas.
>
> [*Mecca and Medina are holy cities in the Islamic religion.]

1. How can you tell that the sultana was rich?

_____

_____

_____

2. How can you tell that religion was a large part of the sultana's life?

_____

_____

_____

3. How does this change your opinion of what a sultana's life was like? Give examples.

_____

_____

_____

4. What do you think "prudent" means? Use a dictionary to help you.

_____

_____

_____

5. What economic issues related to her household did the sultana discuss her will?

_____

_____

_____

A. COMPREHENSION

Circle the letter of the best answer for each question.

1. What part of the world was not included in the Ottoman Empire?
   - **a.** the Middle East
   - **b.** the Balkans
   - **c.** southern India
   - **d.** Asia Minor

2. Which group did Beyazit I defeat in Kosovo?
   - **a.** the Teutonic Knights
   - **b.** the Hungarian army
   - **c.** local Turkish chiefs
   - **d.** the Serbian army

3. How did sultans express their religious beliefs and power?
   - **a.** They built mosques to claim that God willed their rule.
   - **b.** They forced Jews to convert to Islam.
   - **c.** They exiled Christians from Muslim regions.
   - **d.** They had children with only Muslim women.

4. Which group had the legal right to limit the power of sultans?
   - **a.** the Janissaries
   - **b.** the Valide Sultans
   - **c.** the Ulema
   - **d.** the *dhimmis*

5. The capture of which city marked the end of the Byzantine Empire?
   - **a.** Manzikert
   - **b.** Ankara
   - **c.** Kosovo
   - **d.** Constantinople

B. SHORT ANSWER

Write two or three sentences to answer each question.

6. Why was there often much bloodshed after a sultan died?

   _____

   _____

7. Why did Christians and the Ottomans disagree about the *devsirme*?

   _____

   _____

C. ESSAY

On a separate sheet of paper, describe the achievements of the following sultans: Beyazit "the Thunderbolt," Mehmet I, and Mehmet II, "the Conqueror." Explain their similarities and differences.

WHEN TENTS BECOME TOWERS: THE SULTANS SETTLE DOWN
PAGES 83–94

FOR HOMEWORK

STUDENT STUDY GUIDE

pages 35–38

CHAPTER SUMMARY

The Ottoman sultan Suleyman ruled over the empire's Golden Age, and Istanbul flourished as its capital. Suleyman continued to expand the empire, but faced obstacles in attempting to bring more of Europe under its control. After his death, internal and external difficulties and conflicts developed and rule of this vast empire began to weaken.

PERFORMANCE OBJECTIVES

► To describe the reign of Suleyman, his expansion of the Ottoman Empire, and the rebuilding and establishment of Istanbul as the empire's capital

► To understand the influence of European innovations and ideas upon Turkish culture

► To explain the conflicts within the Ottoman Empire between rulers and Janissaries

BUILDING BACKGROUND

Brainstorm a list of factors that helped empires expand and flourish, such as strong leadership, an effective military, and cultural practices that brought people together. Explain that they will learn about how the Ottoman Empire grew under the reign of the sultan Suleyman, but that over time, some of the factors that brought the Ottoman Empire its power also caused it to weaken.

CAST OF CHARACTERS

Suleyman (soo-lay-MAHN) **the Magnificent** sultan of the Ottoman Empire during its Golden Age

Selim (she-LEEM) **"the Grim"** sultan of the Ottoman Empire, father of Suleyman

Mimar (mee-MAHR) **Sinan** (see-NAHN) chief architect of the Ottoman Empire

Ahmet (ah-MEHT) **III** Ottoman sultan of the Tulip Era

VOCABULARY

strait a narrow passage of water joining two larger bodies of water

campaign a series of military operations with a specific goal

siege the surrounding of a city or town in order to capture it; also a long period of adversity

succession the sequence in which one person follows another as ruler

perimeter a boundary protecting a military position

As needed, have students consult the glossary to define the following words: *ablution, Kanun-I-Osman, minaret, mercenary.*

WORKING WITH PRIMARY SOURCES

Point out the quotation from a European ambassador on Student Edition page 84. Discuss what the quotation describes about the importance of a capital city. Explain or elicit that past civilizations also found Istanbul's site to be a good location for their capital. Encourage students to make connections about past and present capital cities.

GEOGRAPHY CONNECTION

Location   Have students locate Turkey on a map, either online or in an atlas. Point out the Dardenelles and the Bosphorus. Discuss how control of these narrow waterways would affect sea trade to the north and the south.

READING COMPREHENSION QUESTIONS

1. How did the establishment of Istanbul as capital bring changes to the Turks? (*Istanbul became a place for the Turks and their sultans to settle.*)

2. What factors limited the spread of the Ottoman Empire in Central Europe? (*The empire had expanded so much that control became more difficult, and further expansion was hampered by weather and change of seasons.*)

3. How did the architect Sinan help establish the Ottoman presence? (*He designed and built many mosques and surrounding complexes that still stand as monuments to the strength of the Ottoman Empire.*)

4. Why was the Ottoman siege of Vienna ultimately unsuccessful? (*The long wait and military inaction allowed the Europeans to construct combined forces that were able to defeat them.*)

5. How was Ahmet III influenced by European culture? (*He was intrigued by European ideas and advances, and brought a less formal style to Ottoman rule.*)

CRITICAL THINKING QUESTIONS

1. How did Suleyman's many talents make him an effective ruler? (*He was a successful military leader, a poet and supporter of the arts, and he created a system of laws for his empire.*)

2. Why did the "dilemma of succession" continue to be a problem for the Ottoman Empire? (*Choosing a ruler was a continual source of conflict for the sultans and their sons, and ineffective rulers began to weaken the empire after the death of Suleyman.*)

3. What roles did the Janissaries play in both strengthening and weakening the Ottoman Empire? (*Janissaries were responsible for many military successes, but they grew less respectful of sultans over time. Tensions over change brought revolts and discontent, which weakened the empire over time.*)

SOCIAL SCIENCES

Economics   The "tulip mania" that began in the Netherlands in the early 1600s offers a clear example of the benefits and dangers of a speculative market. By about 1610, a single rare bulb was used as a bride's dowry. The tulip market crashed almost overnight in 1637. Invite students to research the economics of the tulip craze at *www.bulb.com/historymyth/gardenersfollow.asp*. Have volunteers prepare an oral report to share their findings.

READING AND LANGUAGE ARTS

Reading Nonfiction   Have students examine the events and outcomes of Ottoman military endeavors, such as the Battle of Mohacs and the siege of Vienna. Invite small groups to create a cause-and-effect chain that describes Ottoman successes and failures. This activity may be used as an assessment of students' understanding of chapter content.

Using Language   Encourage students to find examples of exaggeration and superlative language used in primary sources in the chapter, such as a grand vizier's description of the resources of the Ottoman fleet on Student Edition page 91. Discuss the reasons exaggeration is used in each example.

THEN and NOW

The Ottomans made Istanbul a grand capital city. Istanbul today reflects its mix of cultures—divided by the Bosphorus Strait, the western side of Istanbul is European, and the eastern side shows its Asian influences.

LINKING DISCIPLINES

Mathematics Explain that the Islamic tradition of not having statues led to greater use of alternative designs, including geometrics, and that symmetry and geometric shapes guided the work of the architect Sinan. Have students learn more about his work and Ottoman architecture in Istanbul at *www.theottomans.org/ english/art_culture/Ist anbul_5asp*. They can share their findings in an oral report.

WRITING

Interview Encourage students to find examples of exaggeration and superlative language used in primary sources in the chapter, such as a grand vizier's description of the resources of the Ottoman fleet on Student Edition page 91. Discuss the reasons exaggeration is used in each example.

SUPPORTING LEARNING

English Language Learners In small groups of mixed levels of proficiency, have students scan the chapter to find and list words and terms about war and the military. Students can then create categories, such as *Plans*, *Actions*, and *Military People*, and classify the words from their lists.

Struggling Readers Have pairs or small groups of students work together to create a chart that shows Ottoman victories and defeats. Students may want to include dates, leaders, and outcomes.

EXTENDING LEARNING

Enrichment Invite students to investigate Ottoman poetry forms at sites such as *www.poetry-portal.com/poets22html*. Have students prepare poetry readings to share their findings with the class.

Extension Janissaries played many key roles in the history of the Ottoman Empire. Have small groups of students write and present a conversation among Janissaries in which they discuss their point of view towards various leaders, such as Suleyman, Ibrahim, Kara Mustafa, and Ahmet III.

NAME _____ **DATE** _____

COFFEE BREAK

Directions

The following is from _The Medieval & Early Modern World Primary Sources and Reference Volume_, pages 115–116. The passage is from a book about coffee written by the French traveler and scholar Antoine Galland in 1699. In it, he describes the development of coffeehouses and their role in Turkish society. Read the passage and answer the questions that follow.

> These establishments which the Turks called in their language Cahveh Khanch—coffee houses—
> were at first frequented by studious people, those who went to pass a few hours with their
> friends and who formed in the cafés groups of twenty or thirty people who entertained one
> another while having a cup of coffee. When the conversation slowed down, some read from a
> book or, because in those days one found a number of poets in the houses, someone would
> recite a new poem that was then either praised or heatedly criticized. Others played checkers
> or backgammon.
>
> These groups passed unnoticed at the beginning but gradually became better known and
> the novelty, curiosity, and idleness slowly attracted young people finishing their studies and
> about to enter the legal profession, the out-of-work Cadis who were in Constantinople to seek
> reassignment to their post or to find a new job; the Muderis or professors who came to relax,
> and other sorts of people, who living from their investments, found more pleasure in this
> company than in remaining alone at home with nothing to do. Eventually, the coffee houses
> had such a grand reputation who one finds there not only lowly government officials but the
> Pashas and grand nobility around the Sultan, and it was at this moment that there grew to be
> many coffee houses in various neighborhoods of this great city.

1. Who were the first types of people who spent time in coffeehouses?

_____

_____

_____

2. How did the patrons of coffeehouses change over time?

_____

_____

_____

3. How might this account relate to the Tulip Period ruled by Ahmet III?

_____

_____

_____

4. Does the author's description remind you of modern coffeehouses? Explain your response.

_____

_____

_____

CAMEL TRAIN TO MECCA

Directions

This document describing an estimate of funds needed to pay for a religious pilgrimage to Mecca also appears on Student Edition page 90. Read the description, and answer the questions that follow.

> To ensure the safe departure and return, with God's help of the joyful pilgrims who will travel in 1749 on the Damascus pilgrimage route under the supervision of the present governor of Damascus and commander of the pilgrimage, Hacci Esat Pasha, the following expenses are recorded: wages and extras for 1,500 mercenary foot soldiers and cavalrymen, camels and other expenses, rentals of camels for 400 Damascus local troops, basic and supplementary payments to Arab tribes [bribes to keep them from raiding]. . . . Accordingly, upon your excellency's approval, these will be recorded in the chief comptroller's office and the necessary certificates, copies, and orders pertaining to the stated sums will be written. Orders to proceed are requested from your excellency.

1. How would you describe the author's tone? Why do you think he may have used this tone?

_____

_____

_____

2. Why do you think the estimate calls for so many soldiers and cavalrymen?

_____

_____

_____

3. What does the reference to payments to Arab tribes tell you about this practice?

_____

_____

_____

4. Why do you think the author explains how bookkeeping records of the journey's expenses will be kept?

_____

_____

_____

5. Why would the Ottomans go to all the extra expense and trouble to guard the pilgrims?

_____

_____

_____

A. COMPREHENSION

Circle the letter of the best answer for each question.

1. In what way did Suleyman's mother, Hafisa Khatoun, affect the plans of Selim "the Grim" to kill their son?
   a. Her actions helped the plan to succeed.
   b. Her actions accidentally caused the plan to fail.
   c. Her actions prevented the plan from succeeding.
   d. Her actions caused Selim "the Grim" to change his mind about the killing.

2. How did Suleyman's choice of a successor affect the empire?
   a. Selim followed in his father's footsteps and continued to expand the empire.
   b. Selim was an ineffective leader and caused the empire to begin to weaken.
   c. Selim preferred European culture and his ideas brought unrest to the empire.
   d. Selim abolished the Janissaries after they revolted against him.

3. Which of the following describes a Turkish loss in 1683?
   a. the Battle of Lepanto
   b. the retaking of Buda by Christian troops
   c. the Battle of Mohacs
   d. the battle that ended the Turkish siege of Vienna

4. Why were European advances, such as the printing press, considered dangerous by some in the Ottoman Empire?
   a. The Qu'ran had warned against these ideas and technologies, and many Muslims felt that they would bring destruction.
   b. Ottoman rulers felt that relying on European ideas and advances would bring European control.
   c. The books produced by printing presses related only to Christian ideas.
   d. Ottoman rulers felt that books were dangerous because they brought education to so many people.

B. SUMMARIZE

Write a summary of the reign of Ahmet III and tell how it differed from the rule of previous Ottoman sultans.

_____

_____

_____

_____

_____

_____

_____

C. SUPPORTING AN OPINION

Suleyman was an extraordinary leader with many talents. On a separate sheet of paper, write an essay describing his reign and his accomplishments. Explain what you think was most significant about his leadership. Include details that support your opinion.

CHAPTER 8

STOCKING THE ROYAL SPICE CABINET: THE PORTUGUESE EMPIRE PAGES 95–106

FOR HOMEWORK

STUDENT STUDY GUIDE

pages 39–42

CAST OF CHARACTERS

Da Gama (duh GAH-mah), **Vasco** (VAS-ko) Portuguese captain who reached India by sailing around Africa

Dias (DEE-ush), **Bartolomeu** (bahr-TAHL-AH-mew) Portuguese captain who rounded southern tip of Africa

Henry "the Navigator" Portuguese prince who supported navigation and trade

Philip II king of Spain, sent Armada to attack England

CHAPTER SUMMARY

Exploration and naval power were keys to the building of the Portuguese empire in the 1400s and 1500s. Henry the Navigator set in motion the exploration that would lead to Portugal's developing a new sea route to Asia to profit from the spice trade, extending its empire to include Brazil, and profiting from Brazil's resources. Much of what the Portuguese gained was later lost after Philip II of Spain took the Portuguese throne. Though Portugal became independent again, later kings frittered away the empire's wealth, leaving it with a poor economy.

PERFORMANCE OBJECTIVES

▶ To understand the decline of Muslim rule in the Iberian peninsula

▶ To identify Portuguese voyages of discovery, the locations of these routes, and their impact on world economies and society

▶ To explain Portugal's role in the establishment of trade routes among Portugal, Asia, Africa, and Europe

▶ To describe the exchanges among Europe, Africa, Asia, and the Americas in the 15th and 16th centuries

BUILDING BACKGROUND

Direct students to preview the chapter by reading the title, subtitles, captions, and looking at the illustrations. Ask students to predict what this chapter will be about and what they will learn about Portugal from reading the text. List predictions on a chart, and invite students to revise them as they read Chapter 8.

VOCABULARY

navigator a person who plots and controls a voyage, as of a ship

exploration the act of making a search for the purpose of discovery

crown rule; position of a monarch

scurvy a disease caused by the lack of vitamin C

treasury a place where funds are received, kept, and paid out

insurrections uprisings; rebellions

WORKING WITH PRIMARY SOURCES

Point out the quotation from Afonso de Albuquerque in the last paragraph on Student Edition page 100. Discuss what the quotation reveals about his motivation for establishing a network of fortified cities for trade.

GEOGRAPHY CONNECTION

Location Have students use a ruler and the map scale to estimate the distance—via ocean routes—from Lisbon to Brazil and from Lisbon to Goa and Malacca. Discuss the possible difficulties that Portugal may have had in maintaining its overseas holdings from so far away.

READING COMPREHENSION QUESTIONS

1. When and how did Muslim control of much of Portugal end? (*In 1249, crusaders going to the Holy Land aided Portugal to push Muslim Arabs out of Portugal.*)

2. What were the main purposes of Vasco Da Gama's trip in 1498? (*to increase Portugal's wealth through trade or conquest, to expand Christianity, and to find a mysterious Christian kingdom said to be in the East*)

3. Why were spices valuable commodities in Europe? (*Europeans needed spices to enhance monotonous diets or to mask the taste of rotting foods, so they were willing to pay a lot for them.*)

4. Why would a ship captain be willing to make a long sea journey to Southeast Asia to pick up and deliver a load of spices to Europe? (*A captain could become very wealthy after delivering a shipload of spices.*)

5. What resources and goods went from Brazil to Europe? (*high-grade sugar, silver, gold, and diamonds*)

CRITICAL THINKING QUESTIONS

1. Why were mapmakers important to Portuguese exploration? (*Possible answer: Explorers could rely on their maps of known areas and then continue exploring from that point on. Explorers could also use the maps to establish trade routes.*)

2. Why was Bartolomeu Dias's voyage of discovery important to Vasco da Gama? (*Dias had proven there was a navigable route around Africa, which made it possible for da Gama to follow that route round the Cape of Good Hope.*)

3. What effects did Spanish rule have on Portugal and its empire? (*Spanish rule brought the Inquisition to Portugal, which resulted in thousands of people being burned at the stake. The Portuguese navy fought with Spain against the English and the Dutch, sustaining heavy losses. Spanish brutality against the Dutch rebounded on the Portuguese, with the Dutch attacking Portugal's trading places. The Dutch East India Company took over most of the Portuguese spice trade.*)

SOCIAL SCIENCES

Science, Technology, and Society   Remind students that mapmakers were part of the Portuguese explorations of the coast of Africa that Henry the Navigator supported. Invite students to learn more about the history of mapmaking, or cartography, and its influence in the development of a new European world view. Have students prepare an oral report to share their findings.

READING AND LANGUAGE ARTS

Reading Nonfiction   As students read Chapter 8, have them outline each subsection by listing the main ideas and important details in each section of the chapter. After reading each section, students can use their notes to summarize their reading. Use this activity to assess students' understanding of chapter content.

Reading Nonfiction   Point out that the author uses several technical terms for ships and parts of ships. Direct students to scan the chapter to list words related to ships. Then have students define the words, looking them up in a dictionary as needed.

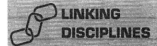

THEN and **NOW**

The Portuguese empire once included holdings in South America, Africa, and Asia. The last of these, Macau, was returned to China in 1999. Today Portugal consists of land on the Iberian Peninsula and the Atlantic islands of the Azores and Madeira.

LINKING DISCIPLINES

Art Have students choose a major building of Portugal to research, including the Batalha Monastery, the Belem Tower, and the Hieryonimites Monastery. Suggest that students describe the building styles, such as Muslim, Renaissance, Baroque, and Gothic, and draw and label architectural features of the building.

WRITING

Explanation Have students use information from Chapter 8 to write an essay that explains why the Portuguese were able to build an empire in the 15th and 16th centuries. Tell students to outline their ideas before they write and to support all statements with facts and examples from the chapter.

SUPPORTING LEARNING

English Language Learners Work with students to identify and define antonyms used to describe the Portuguese empire, such as *huge/small, advantage/disadvantage, and wealth/poverty*. Guide students to use the antonym pairs in sentences about Portugal or its explorations.

Struggling Readers Have students make a two-column chart and in the first column, under the heading *Explorers*, have them list the names of the explorers mentioned in the chapter. In the second column, under the heading *Places Explored*, student should list the places each explorer visited.

EXTENDING LEARNING

Enrichment Invite students to read more of Luis de Camoes's epic poem *The Luciads* in translation. A recent translation by Landeg White is part of the *Oxford World's Classics* series. Allow time for students to share details that reflect the poet's perspectives on Vasco da Gama's pioneer voyage via southern Africa to India, and to analyze those points of view.

Extension Tell students to make a map that shows the goods, ideas, resources, illnesses, and cultural elements that were exchanged among Portugal and various parts of its empire and along Portuguese trade routes in the 15th and 16th centuries. Encourage students to do additional research to gather information for their maps. Allow time for students to explain their maps to the class.

FROM A LETTER BY FERNAO CARDIM

Directions

The following text is from a letter written to Portuguese officials by the Jesuit priest Fernao Cardim, and appears on Student Edition page 106. In it, Fernao Cardim describes the sufferings of the American Indians at the hands of the Portuguese. Read the description with a partner, and answer the questions that follow. If necessary, use a dictionary for help with the meanings of words such as *vexations, rigorous,* and *hewn*.

> . . . "assaults, robberies, captivities and other vexations that always were done to [the Indians], and even now are done. Against the Indians was always a rigorous justice; they have already been hanged, hewn in pieces, quartered." Justice, the priest felt, "will come from Heaven on all the inhabitants of Brazil" for the crimes against the American Indians.

1. What information in the letter is presented as fact and could be verified using other sources?

_____

_____

_____

2. What opinion does Fernao Cardim express in the letter?

_____

_____

_____

3. What effect do you think Fernao Cardim would say that the Portuguese had on the lives of the American Indians? Explain.

_____

_____

_____

4. What does Cardim's use of the word "rigorous" suggest about Portuguese justice against the Indians in Brazil?

_____

_____

_____

5. What was Fernao Cardim's point of view of the way the Portuguese in Brazil treated the Indians? Explain.

_____

_____

_____

6. Why do you think that Cardim chose to use the word "always" in his letter to Portuguese officials?

_____

_____

_____

THE LONGEST JOURNEY

Directions

This excerpt from Gomes Eannes de Zurara's 15th-century *Chronicle of the Discovery and Conquest of Guinea* also appears on Student Edition page 104. In it, Zurara describes a slave auction. Read the excerpt, and answer the questions that follow.

> What heart could be so hard, as not to be pierced with piteous feeling to see that company? For some kept their heads low, and their face bathed in tears, looking one upon another. Others stood groaning very dolorously [sadly], looking up to the height of heaven, fixing their eyes upon it, crying out loudly, as if asking help from the Father of nature; others struck their faces with the palms of their hands, throwing themselves full length upon the ground; while others made lamentations in the manner of a dirge, after the custom of their country. . . .
>
> But to increase their sufferings still more, there now arrived those who had charge of the division of the captives, and . . . then was it needful to part fathers from sons, husbands from wives, brothers from brothers. No respect was shown to either friends nor relations, but each fell where his lot took him, , , ,
>
> Oh, mighty Fortune, who, with thy wheel doest and undoest, compassing the matters of the world as it pleaseth thee, do thou at least put before the eyes of that miserable race some understanding of matters to come, that the captives may receive some consolation in the midst of their great sorrow.

1. How does Gomes Eannes de Zurara make his sympathy for the captives clear?

_____

_____

_____

2. What emotions do you think the captives experienced? Explain.

_____

_____

_____

3. What does Gomes Eannes de Zurara say increased the sufferings of the captives "still more"?

_____

_____

_____

4. What does Zurara's use of the words "No respect was shown to either friends nor relations" suggest about his opinion of those who were in charge of the division of the captives?

_____

_____

_____

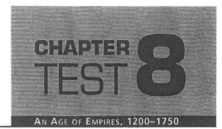
A. COMPREHENSION

Circle the letter of the best answer for each question.

1. Why did Joao build the Batalha Monastery?
   a. The Spanish were victorious over Portugal.
   b. He wanted a monument to Portuguese exploration.
   c. The Portuguese won the Battle of Aljubarrota.
   d. He built it as a tomb for his family.

2. What did Henry the Navigator do to make Portuguese exploration possible?
   a. He sought permission from the rulers of Spain.
   b. He gathered around him a group of mapmakers and men willing to take risks.
   c. He carefully plotted the coast of Africa down to the Cape of Good Hope.
   d. He invented the caravel so that explorers could sail in shallow water.

3. What was the main purpose of Portuguese voyages south along Africa?
   a. slavery   c. missionary work
   b. to deliver spices to India   d. to find a new route to the East

4. Which of the following was **not** brought to Portugal from South America?
   a. slaves   c. silver
   b. sugar   d. diamonds

B. CAUSE AND EFFECT

Complete the chart by writing an effect for each cause.

CAUSE	EFFECT
5. The Portuguese found that they needed only to control outposts, not the interior, for trading.	
6. The Dutch used their faster, well-armed ships to attack Portugal's trading places.	
7. In 1668, insurrections against Spain took place in Portugal.	

C. SUPPORTING AN OPINION

On Student Edition page 102, the author states that "The Hieryonimites Monastery in Lisbon serves as an ideal example of much of this early, lavish time" in Portugal's history. Based on what you have read about the Portuguese empire, do you agree with the author's statement? On a separate sheet of paper, write a paragraph explaining your answer. Use details from the chapter to support your opinion

CHAPTER 9

"GO FURTHER!": SPAIN EXPANDS ACROSS AN OCEAN PAGES 107–119

CAST OF CHARACTERS

Isabella of Castile joint ruler of Spain with Ferdinand

Ferdinand of Aragon joint ruler of Spain with Isabella

Charles V German emperor and (as Charles I), King of Spain

Philip II king of Spain, sent Armada to attack England

Christopher Columbus leader of first known Europeans to reach Americas since Vikings

CHAPTER SUMMARY

The Spanish Empire's goals included establishing profitable colonies and forming a Catholic state. Queen Isabella and King Ferdinand forced Muslims and Jews to convert to Christianity or leave Spain. In 1492 Isabella sponsored Christopher Columbus's voyage to explore the western Atlantic Ocean. Eventually, the Spanish Empire included the Americas and sections of Europe, but it faced challenges from other European countries and from internal weaknesses.

PERFORMANCE OBJECTIVES

- ▶ To explain the decline of Muslim rule in the Iberian Peninsula that culminated in the rise of Spanish kingdoms
- ▶ To know the great voyages of discovery
- ▶ To discuss the exchanges of plants, animals, technology, culture, and ideas among Europe, Africa, Asia, and the Americas

BUILDING BACKGROUND

Elicit from students that parts of the United States were once colonies of Spain, and that many place names come from that time. Discuss what students already know about the Spanish conquest of the Americas, and list their ideas on the chalkboard. Retain the list, and after they read the chapter ask students to note any misconceptions they may have had.

VOCABULARY

Iberian Peninsula the peninsula making up Portugal and Spain

irrigation the process of supplying dry land with water by using ditches, pipes, or streams

Inquisition a trial held by the Roman Catholic Church to suppress heresy

trade winds prevailing winds that blow northeasterly in the Northern Hemisphere and southeasterly in the Southern Hemisphere

conquistadors leaders of the Spanish conquest of America in the 16th century

converso Spanish word for Jews who converted to Christianity

As needed, have students consult the glossary to define the following words: *moriscos, Reformation*.

WORKING WITH PRIMARY SOURCES

Have students examine the 16th-century map of Santo Domingo on Student Edition page 114. Encourage them to speculate how Europeans might be persuaded to move to the colony, based on details from the map.

GEOGRAPHY CONNECTION

Location Make sure students connect the inset map to the outline of the same area on the larger map on Student Edition page 108 Ask students to locate the territory formed after the marriage of Queen Isabella of Castile and King Ferdinand of Aragon.

READING COMPREHENSION QUESTIONS

1. What territory did Charles V rule? (*He ruled Spain, much of Italy and the Netherlands, and he was the leader of the German states. He also ruled "New World" territories.*)

2. How did the Spanish slave trade affect the movements of populations in Africa and Spain? (*Millions of Africans were forcibly taken to the Americas, and hundreds of thousands of impoverished Spaniards left Spain hoping to find wealth and better lives in the Spanish colonies.*)

3. What three events changed the course of Spanish history in 1492? (*Ferdinand and Isabella took the Muslim-held city of Granada and forced the Muslims to convert or leave; they forced the Jews to convert or leave; Isabella sponsored Columbus's voyage to the western Atlantic.*)

4. What was the purpose of the Inquisition? (*to make sure newly converted subjects and other Catholics followed official Catholic doctrine*)

5. What hardships did Native Americans face after colonization? (*The Spanish mistreated Native American laborers; many died of European diseases.*)

CRITICAL THINKING QUESTIONS

1. How did Queen Isabella's travels strengthen the Spanish Empire? (*She got the support from local lords and created a wider network of advisors.*)

2. Why did Christian Spaniards support the Inquisition? (*They had strong religious beliefs.*)

3. Do you agree with the author's opinion that the Jews faced poor conditions whether they left Spain or converted to Christianity? Provide information to support your point of view. (*Possible answers: Yes; if they left they lost any wealth they had; if they stayed they were spied on. No; if they went to the Ottoman Empire there was more economic opportunity.*)

4. How did religious beliefs influence Philip's decision to invade England? (*He believed that England was a "heretic" nation.*)

SOCIAL SCIENCES

Civics Have students make a diagram showing the separate councils of state and parliaments among the Spanish kingdoms of Castile, Aragon, Catalonia, and Valencia during the rule of Ferdinand of Aragon and Isabella of Castile. One useful site is *http://countrystudies.us/spain/7.htm*.

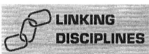

THEN and **NOW**

The History of Don Quixote has influenced the English language. Today the word quixotic (kwik-SOT-ik) describes a person who, like Don Quixote, is impulsive and caught up in the pursuit of unreachable goals.

LINKING DISCIPLINES

Science Instruct students to research the influence of the trade winds on the world's weather and climate and prepare an oral presentation. They may wish to make a map or a diagram showing the movement of the trade winds. Suggest that they look at http://geography. about.com/library/wee kly/aa110200a.htm.

READING AND LANGUAGE ARTS

Reading Nonfiction This chapter describes the effects of the Spanish monarchs' decisions. Have students identify cause-and-effect relationships related to each Spanish ruler.

Using Language Point out to students the saying on page 107 *the saddle was the throne of Spain.* Elicit that this saying implies that in-person communication was better than long-distance communication. Have students brainstorm a new figurative phrase to describe another aspect of Spanish rule.

WRITING

Write a Persuasive Response Have students write a persuasive response to the sermon on page 116, given by Reginaldo de Montesinos. They can write from the point of view of someone who heard the sermon. Remind them to state a clear position in support of a proposition or a proposal. Use this activity to assess students' understanding of the impact of colonization in the Americas.

SUPPORTING LEARNING

English Language Learners Encourage students who are fluent in Spanish to help non-Spanish speakers pronounce the Spanish words in the chapter. Help them use their knowledge of the Spanish terms to understand the English definitions.

Struggling Readers Direct students to create a two-column chart to note details about the Spanish Empire. The categories listed in the left column of the chart can include *Government, Religion and Society, Exploration, Colonization, and Warfare in Europe.*

EXTENDING LEARNING

Enrichment Ask students to read aloud a portion of *The History of Don Quixote de la Mancha* as Reader's Theatre and discuss it afterward. You may wish to provide the excerpt that appears in *The Medieval & Early Modern World Primary Sources and Reference Volume,* pages 103–105. For students who need a greater challenge, the entire novel is found online at *www.online-literature.com/ cervantes/don_quixote/.*

Extension Invite small groups of students to make a multimedia display that highlights the arts and architecture in the Spanish Empire. Suggest they include examples from Muslim architecture through the Golden Age of Spanish Painting.

NAME   DATE

THE SPANISH EMPIRE, 1550–1700

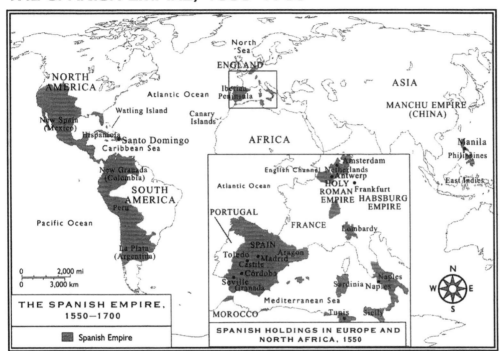

Directions

Use the map and the information in the chapter to answer the questions that follow.

1. What were the names of the Spanish colonies in South America?

_____

_____

2. What does the inset map show?

_____

_____

3. Look at the large map and the inset map. Which city marked on the map was farthest from Seville, Spain?

_____

_____

4. What might have been the challenge of ruling such a large empire?

_____

_____

5. Describe the directions Spanish Armada might have taken if it sailed directly from Spain to the Netherlands to England.

_____

_____

_____

MAN OF LA MANCHA

Directions

The following text is from *The Medieval & Early Modern World Primary Sources and Reference Volume*, pages 103–105. It is an excerpt from Miguel de Cervantes' *Don Quixote*. It is a novel about an aging warrior who sets out, with his squire Sancho Panza, to fulfill his imagined knightly ideals and to improve the world. Read the excerpt with a partner, and answer the questions that follow.

> They caught sight of thirty or forty windmills standing on the plain, and as soon as Don Quixote saw them he said to his squire:
> "Fortune is directing our affairs even better than we could have wished: for you can see over there, good friend Sancho Panza, a place where stand thirty or more monstrous giants with whom I intend to fight a battle and whose lives I intend to take; and with the booty we shall begin to prosper. For this is a just war, and it is a great service to God to wipe such a wicked breed from the face of the earth."
> "What giants?" said Sancho Panza.
> "Those giants that you can see over there," replied his master "with long arms: there are giants with arms almost six miles long."
> "Look you here," Sancho retorted, "those over there aren't giants, they're windmills and what look to you like arms are sails—when the wind turns them they make the millstones go round."
> "It is perfectly clear," replied Don Quixote, "that you are but a raw novice in this matter of adventures. They are giants; and if you are frightened, you can take yourself away and say your prayer while I engage them in fierce and arduous combat."

1. What do you think Don Quixote is like?

_____

_____

_____

2. What can you tell about life in Spain, based on this excerpt from the novel?

_____

_____

_____

3. What is humorous about this passage?

_____

_____

_____

4. How does this excerpt help you understand some of the values or beliefs in Spanish society at this time? Is the author critical of these values?

_____

_____

_____

NAME _____ **DATE** _____

A. COMPREHENSION

Circle the letter of the best answer to each question.

1. Why did Isabella and Ferdinand travel throughout Spain?
   a. to meet powerful, land-owning nobles
   b. to collect the names of Muslims who refused to convert
   c. to give funding to Catholic churches
   d. to build a new network of trusted advisors

2. What event did not take place in 1492?
   a. the introduction of the Inquisition to Spain
   b. Ferdinand and Isabella's capture of the city of Grenada
   c. Christopher Columbus's journey to the western Atlantic
   d. Ferdinand and Isabella's decision to expel Jews who refused to convert

3. What contributions did Jews make to Spanish society?
   a. They brought fruit crops grown using irrigation.
   b. They took part in the Golden Age of Spanish Painting.
   c. They translated from Arabic many Greek and Roman texts.
   d. They introduced the silk industry to Spain.

4. What was **not** a reason why the English defeated the Spanish Armada?
   a. The English were able to burn some of the Spanish ships.
   b. The English had longer-range guns.
   c. A North Sea storm sank some of the Spanish fleet.
   d. The Spanish did not have a very large fleet.

B. SHORT ANSWER

Write two or three sentences to answer each question.

5. What was the purpose of the Inquisition? _____

_____

6. What was the purpose of the mission system in the Americas? _____

_____

C. CAUSE AND EFFECT

Complete the chart by writing an effect for each cause.

CAUSE	EFFECT
7. The Europeans brought to the Americas smallpox, measles, mumps, yellow fever, and other new diseases.	
8. The Spanish did not develop their resources and ignored new technologies.	
9. The Pueblo Indians did not like the way they were treated by the Franciscan missionaries.	

THE WEDDING RING EMPIRE: EUROPE UNDER THE HABSBURGS   PAGES 120–132

FOR HOMEWORK

STUDENT STUDY GUIDE

pages 47–50

CAST OF CHARACTERS

Johannes Kepler astronomer who discovered that planets moved in elliptical paths

Albrecht von Wallenstein Habsburg general during the Thirty Years' War

Eugene of Savoy Habsburg general who led army against Ottomans

Maria Theresa Habsburg ruler; began military, tax, and education reforms

CHAPTER SUMMARY

The Habsburg Empire lasted for 500 years by using royal marriages to build and expand their territories to rule much of central Europe. Religious conflict led them into the Thirty Years' War, and the Habsburgs also fought off Ottoman invasions. During the reign of Maria Theresa, new alliances and reforms took place, but conflict over religion and direction continued to threaten the empire's viability.

PERFORMANCE OBJECTIVES

▶ To describe the role of the Catholic church in politics in the Habsburg Empire

▶ To analyze the sources of religious conflict in the Habsburg Empire

▶ To understand Johannes Kepler's contributions to the field of astronomy

▶ To describe the strengths and weaknesses of Habsburg rulers

BUILDING BACKGROUND

Lead a discussion to elicit that most empires expanded their territories through military campaigns. Then point out the quotation on Student Edition page 120, "Let the strong fight wars. You, happy Austria, marry!" and discuss how some empires grew through royal marriages. Conduct a "chapter walk" to preview chapter content and guide students to see that royal marriages did not necessarily lead to a strong empire—or even a happy one.

VOCABULARY

traits distinguishing physical features or personality characteristics

holdings lands that are owned or possessed

elliptical paths a movement that forms an ellipse, or oval shape

discrimination an act or actions based on prejudice

assassins those who plot to murder, especially of a public official

mercenary soldiers paid to fight for another country

insignia a distinguishing sign, emblem, or symbol

As needed, have students consult the glossary to define the following terms: *cuius regio, eius religio, Ladies Peace, kuruc.*

WORKING WITH PRIMARY SOURCES

Point out the page from the Treaty of Westphalia on Student Edition page 125. Explain that the Treaty of Westphalia marks the origination of modern nation-states. Invite students to learn more about this important document at *http://en.wikipedia.org/wiki/Treaty_of_Westphalia.*

GEOGRAPHY CONNECTION

Location Have students locate Austria on the map on Student Edition page 121. Discuss the advantages and disadvantages of its location as the center of the Habsburg Empire.

READING COMPREHENSION QUESTIONS

1. What role did religion play in the Habsburg Empire? (*The Habsburgs were loyal Catholics and worked against reforms; this conflict led to the Thirty Years' War.*)

2. What did Kepler determine about planetary orbits? (*He determined that planets did not move in circles, but in paths that were more like ovals.*)

3. Describe the leadership of General Wallenstein during the Thirty Years' War, and explain why the emperor had him assassinated. (*He was a strong leader and a good strategist. Ferdinand had him assassinated because he felt that Wallenstein was working against him.*)

4. What role did Eugene of Savoy play in the Habsburg Empire? (*He led the Habsburg Empire in their defeat of Ottoman invasions and other wars that threatened to weaken the empire.*)

5. What challenges did Maria Theresa face when she came to lead the Habsburg Empire? (*She had to establish herself as a legitimate leader; she had to form new alliances and lead wars against the Prussians; she decided to institute reforms within her empire.*)

CRITICAL THINKING QUESTIONS

1. How did the death of Jan Hus illustrate the power of the Habsburg emperor? (*Seeking religious reforms, Hus believed that he would be free to voice his concerns, but he was labeled a heretic and burned at the stake. This shows that the emperor had strong links to the Catholic Church, was accountable to no one, and could make any decision he liked.*)

2. How was the Peace of Augsburg similar to the Treaty of Westphalia? (*Both centered on the idea that a ruler could determine the religion of his lands.*)

3. What gave Hapsburg leaders strength? What were their weaknesses? (*Habsburg leaders found strength in their religious beliefs and their ability to gain and hold power through their families. Many of them failed to look beyond their own interests and were often inattentive or passive when they needed to be decisive.*)

SOCIAL SCIENCES

Economics The author states that during Maria Theresa's reign, the peasantry kept only three-fifths of their wages. In 2002, 24 percent of the average single person's wages in the United States went to income taxes and Social Security. Work with students to consult almanacs and other resources to determine the average tax burden in other countries and see how the United States compares. Have students work in small groups to create charts that show the comparison.

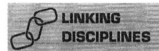

THEN and **NOW**

As the capital of the Habsburg Empire, Vienna became a showcase for culture and the arts. Vienna's deep and enduring appreciation for culture is still evident today in its year-round music festivals and outstanding museums.

LINKING DISCIPLINES

Science The "Habsburg jaw" common to many of the members of this royal family provides an entry for investigations in the field of genetics. Gregor Mendel, an Austrian monk and botanist, was a pioneer in this area. Have students use print and electronic resources to learn more about Mendel's work and present their findings to the class.

LITERATURE CONNECTION

There are numerous enjoyable books that will broaden students' knowledge of Habsburg Empire.

Banville, John. *Kepler: A Novel*. Vintage, 1993. Historical Fiction. Kepler's story contrasts the chaos of his personal life with the order he sought to find through astronomy. AVERAGE

Bonney, Richard. *The Thirty Years' War*. Osprey Publishing, 2002. Nonfiction. The story of the Thirty Years' War includes both military and human costs. AVERAGE

Crankshaw, Edward. *Maria Theresa*. Atheneum, 1986. Biography. The story of Maria Theresa ranges from military battles to a love of music. ADVANCED

READING AND LANGUAGE ARTS

Reading Nonfiction Point out the sidebar quotation from Johannes Kepler on Student Edition page 122. Discuss how the quotation provides details on Kepler that make him more real to the reader. Invite students to examine other sidebars in the chapter and discuss their purposes.

Using Language On Student Edition page 120, the author says that the Habsburg Empire was "like a house that was continually being remodeled," and also "like a family business." Have students identify a simile the author uses about the emperor on page 121 and discuss how this and the previous similes help establish a general understanding of how the Habsburg Empire functioned.

WRITING

Dialogue Have students write a dialogue between Maria Theresa and one of her advisors. The dialogue should outline at least two issues she faced and the courses of action she pursued to address these issues. Use this activity to assess students' understanding of problems and solutions in the Habsburg Empire.

SUPPORTING LEARNING

English Language Learners Have students work independently or in pairs to look for words ending in *-ly* on Student Edition pages 125–126. Tell students to identify the base, or root, in each word they identify. Explain or elicit that the addition of the suffix *-ly* changes the word's part of speech, and then develop sentences using both the base word and the word with the *-ly* suffix.

Struggling Readers As they read, have students monitor their comprehension by stopping and writing questions that restate main ideas, such as *What problems did the Habsburg Empire face?* Later, have pairs or small groups share and answer their questions.

EXTENDING LEARNING

Enrichment Johannes Kepler's work confirmed the previous findings of Copernicus, and later influenced the work of Isaac Newton. He also made advances in the studies of optics and the eye. Encourage students to use Internet and library resources to research one aspect of Kepler's work and present their findings to the class in an oral report.

Extension Have students write and present a panel discussion among Habsburg rulers of different times. Each ruler should explain the challenges he or she faced, and how he or she dealt with these issues.

LITERACY TIPS

In addition to using the suggestions in the Supporting Learning and Extending Learning sections, refer back frequently to pages 16–19 for strategies and advice from a literacy coach.

NAME   **DATE**

THE HABSBURG EMPIRE, 1700S

Directions

Use the map to answer the questions that follow.

1. Which cities shown on the map were part of the Habsburg Empire?

_____

_____

2. Use the scale of miles to determine the distance between Prague and Vienna.

_____

_____

3. Which geographic features did the Ottoman Empire need to consider when planning to invade the Habsburg Empire?

_____

_____

4. What geographic advantage did Vienna, Buda, and Pest offer the Habsburg Empire?

_____

_____

5. Why do you think it was important that the Habsburg Empire extended as far south as northern Italy and Croatia?

_____

_____

EUGENE OF SAVOY

Directions

Eugene of Savoy's "mysterious past" caused him to fight against the French, and he became a general for the Habsburgs. The following remarks by and about Eugene of Savoy also appear on Student Edition pages 127 and 128. Read the statements and then answer the questions that follow.

Eugene then went to the Habsburgs and took revenge by beating Louis's armies. After one raid on French soil, Eugene said to a friend, "Didn't I say I would only return to France, sword in hand?"

The problems of Europe, Eugene wrote sarcastically to a friend, "certainly disturbed the Emperor [Leopold] for the space of an hour. But luckily on the same day, there was a procession, and he forgot anything else."

Duke of Marbourgh, amazed by the general's successes, wrote of him, "Why did the Prince consider so many possibilities when one was enough for victory?"

1. What does the first quotation tell you about Eugene of Savoy's motivation in fighting for the Habsburg Empire?

_____

_____

_____

_____

2. What do Eugene's remarks in the second quotation reveal about his opinion of Emperor Leopold?

_____

_____

_____

_____

3. Eugene served under three Habsburg emperors. Why do you think he continued to fight for them?

_____

_____

_____

_____

4. How does the third quotation support the idea that Eugene was a remarkable military leader?

_____

_____

_____

_____

NAME   **DATE**

A. COMPREHENSION

Circle the letter of the best answer for each question.

1. The Habsburg Empire is also known as the wedding ring empire because
   a. it marked a time of peace and cooperation between European lands.
   b. royal marriages persuaded its people to unite under a single religion.
   c. successors to the throne wore a special ring.
   d. royal marriages helped the empire expand and strengthen.

2. The religious beliefs of Habsburg rulers were marked by
   a. a willingness to move towards tolerance and reform.
   b. a strong desire to preserve Catholicism.
   c. efforts to weaken the control of the Holy Roman Empire.
   d. encouraging the rise of Protestantism.

3. The Treaty of Westphalia meant that
   a. individuals were legally free to follow their own religious beliefs.
   b. Catholic leaders would begin to institute religious reforms.
   c. rulers could determine the religion of the lands they ruled.
   d. Catholicism was the only accepted religion within the Habsburg Empire.

4. Under the leadership of Eugene of Savoy,
   a. a peaceful end came to the Thirty Years' War, and Central European states united under the Habsburg Empire.
   b. Habsburg rulers came to understand that using the resources of their lands was more important than adding new territories.
   c. France was invaded and became a part of the Habsburg Empire.
   d. the Ottomans were held back from Central Europe and Habsburg rule was strengthened in their holdings.

5. A problem that Maria Theresa did not have to face during her reign was
   a. the refusal by Hungary to support the empire.
   b. the growing power of the Prussians.
   c. the need for societal and educational reform.
   d. a need to establish herself as the legitimate successor to Charles VI.

B. MAIN IDEA AND DETAILS

On a separate sheet of paper, write an essay that explains the importance of Johannes Kepler's work, and what role religion played in his life as in the Habsburg Empire. Include details that support your ideas.

CHAPTER SUMMARY

The Manchu of northeastern China ruled China after the disastrous end of the Ming dynasty. As a minority, the Manchu kept their language and clan system, and they closed Manchuria to Chinese settlement. They tried to maintain their religion, class structure, and marriage customs. Within China, the Manchu allowed people to follow Confucian ideas and Buddhist beliefs. Kangxi and Qianlong were two of the most successful Qing emperors. They expanded the borders of China and supported trade with other countries.

PERFORMANCE OBJECTIVES

▶ To understand the effects of the reopening of the ancient Silk Road between Europe and China
▶ To discuss the exchanges of plants, animals, technology, culture, and ideas among Europe, Africa, Asia, and the Americas

BUILDING BACKGROUND

Explain that this chapter describes how a minority group called the Manchu ruled China. Write minority rule on the board. Work with students to predict problems that the government might have faced while trying to control a majority culture.

**CAST OF
CHARACTERS**

Kangxi (kahng-shee)
Qing emperor of China
Qianlong (chyen-loong)
Qing emperor of China

VOCABULARY

dynasty succession of rulers from the same family or line

administration the act of managing a government or institution

customs practices followed by a people of a particular group or region

deity a god or goddess

Buddhist a person who follows the teachings of Buddha

Confucian of the teachings of Confucius, a Chinese philosopher

WORKING WITH PRIMARY SOURCES

Direct students to examine the photograph of the Forbidden City in Beijing on Student Edition page 142. Have them notice the symmetry of the building and grounds. Help them speculate how its imposing appearance might have symbolized the rulers' power.

GEOGRAPHY CONNECTION

Movement Ask students to trace the routes along the Silk Road on the map on Student Edition page 133. Have them identify geographic barriers that might have made travel difficult.

READING COMPREHENSION QUESTIONS

1. What problems did the Ming dynasty leave for the Manchu? (*uncollected taxes, unread reports from neglectful Ming emperors, and inept officials in the palace administration*)

2. Why did the Manchu have difficulties ruling the Chinese people? (*They were outnumbered.*)

3. Why were Chinese men forced to wear their hair in long queues? (*so that the Manchu could show control and identify their enemies*)

4. Was the Manchu class system more rigid or less rigid than the Chinese class system? (*less rigid*)

5. How did Kangxi support his people's well-being? Give an example. (*Possible answer: He supported education and examined the dike system on the Yangzi River.*)

CRITICAL THINKING QUESTIONS

1. Why did the Manchu want to keep their language and clan system? (*They were in the minority, and they wanted to keep their culture intact. They were afraid that they would be overwhelmed by the Chinese and fall, as the Mongols had.*)

2. How were the Manchu able to end the practice of widow suicide? (*The emperor Qianlong restored Buddhist temples dedicated to a goddess believed to comfort as a mother or grandmother might do; this helped people valued older women.*)

3. Why do you think many historians would disagree with the Ming loyalist poets who protested the Manchu rule? (*Possible answer: Perhaps because the two best Qing emperors each ruled for more than 60 years and provided stability to China.*)

4. Why do you think the scholar class might subvert the Manchu? (*Possbile answer: Perhaps because they were educated and could organize a rebellion.*)

SOCIAL SCIENCES

Economics   Corn is native to the Western Hemisphere. By about 1575, farmers were growing corn in western China. Have students research the origin of corn, sweet potatoes, or peanuts and find out how they became part of Chinese agriculture. Suggest they make a flow chart showing what they learn.

READING AND LANGUAGE ARTS

Reading Nonfiction   This chapter compares and contrasts the rule of the Manchu emperors Kangxi and Qianlong. Have students complete a Venn diagram (see reproducibles at the back of this guide) in which they note similarities and differences between the emperors. Use this activity to assess students' understanding of chapter content.

Using Language   Point out the phrase "you didn't mess with Mongols and their horses" on Student Edition page 141. Make sure students can identify the verb *mess* as an example of slang, or informal language. Discuss how using slang in limited amounts can help connect readers to the past. Have students find or suggest other examples of slang that could be used to describe the Manchu.

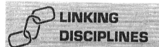

THEN and NOW

Beijing is the second-largest city in China. As the capital of the People's Republic of China, it is the center of government, education, and culture. It also has a thriving industrial base.

LINKING DISCIPLINES

Mathematics
Numbers play an important role in the author's description of Manchu China. Assign partners to write and solve word problems related to Manchu China. Problems might use fractions or percentages to compare the Manchu population to that of China, or they may relate to the number of books in Qianlong's library.

There are numerous enjoyable books that will broaden students' knowledge of Manchu China.

Birch, Cyril. *Chinese Myths and Fantasies.* Oxford University Press Children's Books, 1993. Mythology. This collection includes Chinese myths that explained natural phenomenon. EASY

Ho, Chuimei. *Splendors of China's Forbidden City: The Glorious Reign of Emperor Qianlong.* Merrell Holberton, 2004. Nonfiction. This book reveals long-forgotten works of art collected by the Emperor Qianlong. ADVANCED

Larson, Jeanne. *Manchu Palaces: A Novel.* Henry Holt & Company, 1996. Historical Fiction. The Imperial Court of China's Manchu Qing Dynasty is the setting of this novel. ADVANCED

LITERACY TIPS

In addition to using the suggestions in the Supporting Learning and Extending Learning sections, refer back frequently to pages 16–19 for strategies and advice from a literacy coach.

WRITING

Write a Descriptive Poem   Instruct students to write a descriptive poem about one aspect of life in China during the Qing dynasty. They should include figurative language to convey their ideas.

SUPPORTING LEARNING

English Language Learners   Help students identify how conjunctions link ideas in complex sentences. For example, the words *and, but,* or *or* add information, and the words *after, since,* or *until* show time sequence. Guide students to find examples of both types of conjunctions in the chapter.

Struggling Readers   As students read the chapter, have them pause periodically to ask themselves how the people and events seem similar or different to what they know in today's world, or to other empires they have read about in *An Age of Empires.*

EXTENDING LEARNING

Enrichment   Have students research the role of women during the Qing dynasty. Suggest that they focus on Manchu women or Chinese women. They may wish to write a skit in which pairs of students role-play an interview with a woman from that era.

Extension   Direct small groups of students to make a cultural map of China during the time of the Qing dynasty. Have them shade a historical map of China and its neighbors with the major cultural groups and create a legend.

NAME   **DATE**

THE MANCHU EMPIRE, 1750

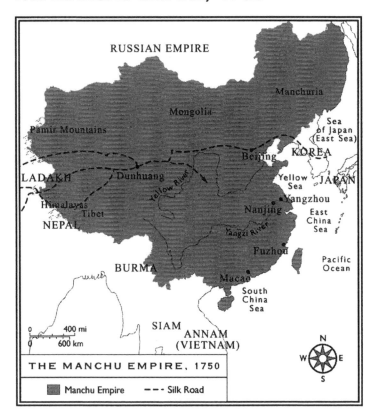

Directions

Use the map and the information in the chapter to answer the questions that follow.

1. What were the geographic barriers along the western border of the empire?

_____

_____

2. What were the Yangzi River and the Yellow River most likely used for?

_____

_____

3. Why do you think Beijing was a major destination along the Silk Road?

_____

_____

4. What made Yangzhou, Nanjing, Fuzhou, and Macao good meeting places for traders?

_____

_____

5. Why do you think the Silk Road branched into separate trails?

_____

_____

NAME   **DATE**

LOOKING OUT FOR THE LITTLE GUY

Directions

This excerpt is from a letter written by a Chinese poet, painter, and calligrapher named Cheng Panch'io. He was also a Qing magistrate who was concerned with providing help to the poor people. The excerpt also appears on Student Edition page 135. Read the excerpt, and answer the questions that follow.

> There is no one in the world who is not a descendant of the Yellow Emperor [the Chinese ancestor]. . . . But today some have unfortunately become slaves, slave girls, concubines, and poor laborers, living in poverty and distress and unable to help themselves; it would be wrong to assume that their ancestors were slaves, slave girls, concubines, and poor laborers in generations ago. Once they make up their minds and are willing to work hard, some of them become rich and honored in their own life time; and others become so in the next generation. Some . . . taunt others on their birth and brag about their previous generations saying, "Who is he, and yet he is high up? I am such and such a person, and yet I am down and out. There is no justice in heaven or in the affairs of man." Also, they do not know that is exactly the justice of heaven and human affairs. . . . His ancestors were poor, and now it is his turn to be rich and honored; your ancestors were rich and honored and now it is your turn to be poor. Again, what is wrong with that?
>
> After I . . . became a government graduate, whenever I found in the old trunks at our home some deed of a slave sold into our family in [a] former generation, I at once burned it over the oil lamp. I did not even return it to the person concerned, for I felt if I did it would be an obvious act and increase the man's embarrassment.

1. What do you think the Chinese believed about their mythological origins?

_____

_____

_____

_____

2. How does Cheng Panch'io feel toward people who are slaves or poor laborers?

_____

_____

_____

_____

3. Does Cheng Panch'io believe that people are destined to stay in one economic class throughout their lives? Explain.

_____

_____

_____

_____

4. Why do you think Cheng Panch'io burned the deed of a slave from a former generation instead of returning it to the person's descendants?

_____

_____

_____

_____

NAME   **DATE**

A. COMPREHENSION

Circle the letter of the best answer for each question.

1. What part of China did the Manchus come from?
   - **a.** the southwest
   - **b.** the northwest
   - **c.** the northeast
   - **d.** the southeast

2. What was a problem faced by Manchu leaders?
   - **a.** They did not have their own written language.
   - **b.** They did not have soldiers who could ride horses.
   - **c.** They did not understand Chinese bureaucracy.
   - **d.** They were outnumbered by the Chinese.

3. What did the Manchu do to protect their culture and society?
   - **a.** They prevented Chinese soldiers from serving in the army.
   - **b.** They isolated China from foreign traders.
   - **c.** They destroyed Chinese art and literature.
   - **d.** They closed Manchuria to Chinese settlement.

4. Which statement is true about the Manchu and Chinese class systems?
   - **a.** Both class systems allowed all groups to intermarry.
   - **b.** The Manchu's class system was more rigid than the Chinese's.
   - **c.** The Chinese class system was more rigid than the Manchu's.
   - **d.** Both class systems said a person's life was determined by birth.

B. CAUSE AND EFFECT

Complete the chart by writing an effect for each cause.

CAUSE	EFFECT
5. The Manchu objected to the practice of widow suicide.	
6. The Manchu wanted to maintain their language.	
7. Qianlong wanted to expand the borders of China.	

C. EXAMINE HISTORICAL AND CULTURAL PERSPECTIVES

Emperor Kangxi was fond of the following passage from the Book of Changes: "When the sun stands at midday, it begins to set, when the moon is full, it begins to wane. The fullness and emptiness of heaven and earth wane and wax in the course of time. How much truer is this of men." Write an essay to describe how the passage might refer to the Manchu Empire and other empires you have studied.

NAME _____ **DATE** _____

Directions
Answer each of the following questions. Use additional paper if necessary

1. Create a cause and effect chart to show how Mongol control affected the Silk Road and its accompanying trade, and how this allowed them to develop a new form of currency.

_____
_____
_____
_____
_____
_____

2. Write a paragraph that describes the contributions of Nicolaus Copernicus and Johannes Kepler to the field of astronomy.

_____
_____
_____
_____
_____

3. Write a paragraph that explains how physical geographic factors contributed to the alliance that formed between Poland and Lithuania in the 14th century. Give one reason that explains why these two lands were unlikely partners.

_____
_____
_____
_____
_____

4. Write a paragraph that lists the reforms and changes the Romanov leaders Alexis, Sophia, and Peter brought to Russia. Describe one reform or change in detail.

_____
_____
_____
_____

5. The Mughal Empire in India expanded Muslim rule. Write a paragraph that describes how religious tolerance in the Mughal Empire encouraged cultural blending.

_____
_____
_____
_____

6. Think about the role of Janissaries in the Ottoman Empire. Then make a two-column chart with the headings *Advantages* and *Disadvantages*. Use the chart to show the positive and negative features of this system.

_____

_____

_____

_____

_____

7. Write a paragraph that tells why Portugal worked so diligently to establish sea routes to India. Include a description of one Portuguese explorer and his accomplishments.

_____

_____

_____

_____

_____

8. Use an outline graphic organizer to list details that support the main idea that life for non-Christians in Spain was changed by the rule of Ferdinand and Isabella.

_____

_____

_____

_____

_____

9. Both the Polish and Lithuanian Commonwealth and the Habsburg Empire relied on royal marriages and religion as ways to expand territories and control lands. Write a paragraph that includes examples of how these factors contributed to the rise of one of the two empires.

_____

_____

_____

_____

_____

10. Horses were important to many peoples and lands, including the Mongols, the Manchu, Lithuania, and Spain. Write an essay that describes the many ways these animals were used during the age of empires. Include a specific example of how they were especially significant to one of the empires.

_____

_____

_____

_____

_____

SCORING RUBRIC

The reproducibles on the following pages have been adapted from this rubric for use as handouts and a student self-scoring activity, with added focus on planning, cooperation, revision and presentation. You may wish to tailor the self-scoring activity—for example, asking students to comment on how low scores could be improved, or focusing only on specific rubric points. Use the Library/Media Center Research Log to help students focus and evaluate their research for projects and assignments.

As with any rubric, you should introduce and explain the rubric before students begin their assignments. The more thoroughly your students understand how they will be evaluated, the better prepared they will be to produce projects that fulfill your expectations.

	ORGANIZATION	CONTENT	ORAL/WRITTEN CONVENTIONS	GROUP PARTICIPATION
4	• Clearly addresses all parts of the writing task. • Demonstrates a clear understanding of purpose and audience. • Maintains a consistent point of view, focus, and organizational structure, including the effective use of transitions. • Includes a clearly presented central idea with relevant facts, details, and/or explanations.	• Demonstrates that the topic was well researched. • Uses only information that was essential and relevant to the topic. • Presents the topic thoroughly and accurately. • Reaches reasonable conclusions clearly based on evidence.	• Contains few, if any, errors in grammar, punctuation, capitalization, or spelling. • Uses a variety of sentence types. • Speaks clearly, using effective volume and intonation.	• Demonstrated high levels of participation and effective decision making. • Planned well and used time efficiently. • Demonstrated ability to negotiate opinions fairly and reach compromise when needed. • Utilized effective visual aids.
3	• Addresses all parts of the writing task. • Demonstrates a general understanding of purpose and audience. • Maintains a mostly consistent point of view, focus, and organizational structure, including the effective use of some transitions. • Presents a central idea with mostly relevant facts, details, and/or explanations.	• Demonstrates that the topic was sufficiently researched. • Uses mainly information that was essential and relevant to the topic. • Presents the topic accurately but leaves some aspects unexplored. • Reaches reasonable conclusions loosely related to evidence.	• Contains some errors in grammar, punctuation, capitalization, or spelling. • Uses a variety of sentence types. • Speaks somewhat clearly, using effective volume and intonation.	• Demonstrated good participation and decision making with few distractions. • Planning and used its time acceptably. • Demonstrated ability to negotiate opinions and compromise with little aggression or unfairness.
2	• Addresses only parts of the writing task. • Demonstrates little understanding of purpose and audience. • Maintains an inconsistent point of view, focus, and/or organizational structure, which may include ineffective or awkward transitions that do not unify important ideas. • Suggests a central idea with limited facts, details, and/or explanations.	• Demonstrates that the topic was minimally researched. • Uses a mix of relevant and irrelevant information. • Presents the topic with some factual errors and leaves some aspects unexplored. • Reaches conclusions that do not stem from evidence presented in the project.	• Contains several errors in grammar, punctuation, capitalization, or spelling. These errors may interfere with the reader's understanding of the writing. • Uses little variety in sentence types. • Speaks unclearly or too quickly. May interfere with the audience's understanding of the project.	• Demonstrated uneven participation or was often off-topic. Task distribution was lopsided. • Did not show a clear plan for the project, and did not use time well. • Allowed one or two opinions to dominate the activity, or had trouble reaching a fair consensus.
1	• Addresses only one part of the writing task. • Demonstrates no understanding of purpose and audience. • Lacks a point of view, focus, organizational structure, and transitions that unify important ideas. • Lacks a central idea but may contain marginally related facts, details, and/or explanations.	• Demonstrates that the topic was poorly researched. • Does not discriminate relevant from irrelevant information. • Presents the topic incompletely, with many factual errors. • Did not reach conclusions.	• Contains serious errors in grammar, punctuation, capitalization, or spelling. These errors interfere with the reader's understanding of the writing. • Uses no sentence variety. • Speaks unclearly. The audience must struggle to understand the project.	• Demonstrated poor participation by the majority of the group. Tasks were completed by a small minority. • Failed to show planning or effective use of time. • Was dominated by a single voice, or allowed hostility to derail the project.

NAME _____ **PROJECT** _____

DATE _____

ORGANIZATION & FOCUS	CONTENT	ORAL/WRITTEN CONVENTIONS	GROUP PARTICIPATION

COMMENTS AND SUGGESTIONS

UNDERSTANDING YOUR SCORE

Organization: Your project should be clear, focused on a main idea, and organized. You should use details and facts to support your main idea.

Content: You should use strong research skills. Your project should be thorough and accurate.

Oral/Written Conventions: For writing projects, you should use good composition, grammar, punctuation, and spelling, with a good variety of sentence types. For oral projects, you should engage the class using good public speaking skills.

Group Participation: Your group should cooperate fairly and use its time well to plan, assign and revise the tasks involved in the project.

NAME _____   **GROUP MEMBERS** _____

_____

_____

_____

Use this worksheet to describe your project by finishing the sentences below.
For individual projects and writing assignments, use the "How I did" section.
For group projects, use both "How I did" and "How we did" sections.

The purpose of this project is to :

Scoring Key =   **4** – extremely well
3 – well
2 – could have been better
1 – not well at all

HOW I DID

I understood the purpose and requirements for this project...

I planned and organized my time and work...

This project showed clear organization that emphasized the central idea...

I supported my point with details and description...

I polished and revised this project...

I utilized correct grammar and good writing/speaking style...

Overall, this project met its purpose...

HOW WE DID

We divided up tasks...

We cooperated and listened to each other...

We talked through what we didn't understand...

We used all our time to make this project the best it could be...

Overall, as a group we worked together...

I contributed and cooperated with the team...

NAME _____

DUE DATE _____

Brainstorm: Other Sources and Places to Look

Places I **Know** to Look

What I Need to **Find**

I need to use:

- [ ] primary
- [ ] secondary

sources.

WHAT I FOUND

Title/Author/Location (call # or URL)

How I Found it

- Suggestion
- Library Catalog
- Browsing
- Internet Search
- Web link

- Primary Source
- Secondary Source

- Book/Periodical
- Website
- Other

Rate each source from 1 (low) to 4 (high) in the categories below

helpful   relevant

GRAPHIC ORGANIZERS

GUIDELINES

Reproducibles of seven different graphic organizers are provided on the following pages. These give your students a variety of ways to sort and order all the information they are receiving in this course. Use the organizers for homework assignments, classroom activities, tests, small group projects, and as ways to help the students take notes as they read.

1. Determine which graphic organizers work best for the content you are teaching. Some are useful for identifying main ideas and details; others work better for making comparisons, and so on.

2. Graphic organizers help students focus on the central points of the lesson while leaving out irrelevant details.

3. Use graphic organizers to give a visual picture of the key ideas you are teaching.

4. Graphic organizers can help students recall important information. Suggest students use them to study for tests.

5. Graphic organizers provide a visual way to show the connections between different content areas.

6. Graphic organizers can enliven traditional lesson plans and encourage greater interactivity within the classroom.

7. Apply graphic organizers to give students a concise, visual way to break down complex ideas.

8. Encourage students to use graphic organizers to identify patterns and clarify their ideas.

9. Graphic organizers stimulate creative thinking in the classroom, in small groups, and for the individual student.

10. Help students determine which graphic organizers work best for their purposes, and encourage them to use graphic organizers collaboratively whenever they can.

11. Help students customize graphic organizers as particular exercises dictate: e.g., more or fewer boxes, lines, or blanks than appear.

OUTLINE

MAIN IDEA: _____

_____

_____

DETAIL: _____

_____

DETAIL: _____

_____

DETAIL: _____

_____

MAIN IDEA: _____

_____

_____

DETAIL: _____

_____

DETAIL: _____

_____

DETAIL: _____

_____

Name _____ Date _____

MAIN IDEA MAP

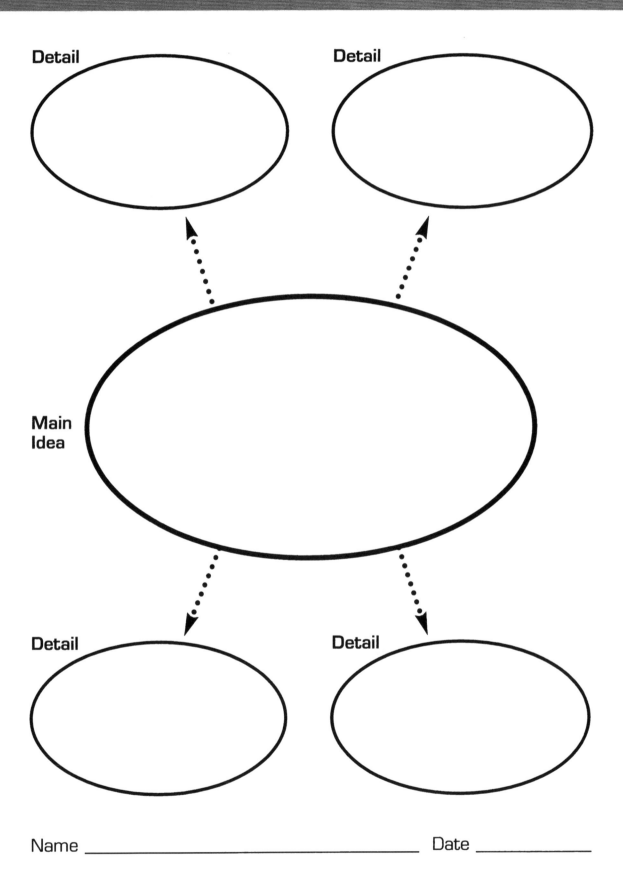

Detail

Detail

Main Idea

Detail

Detail

Name _____ Date _____

K-W-L CHART

K	W	L
What I Know	What I Want to Know	What I Learned

Name _____ Date _____

VENN DIAGRAM

Write differences in the circles. Write similarities where the circles overlap.

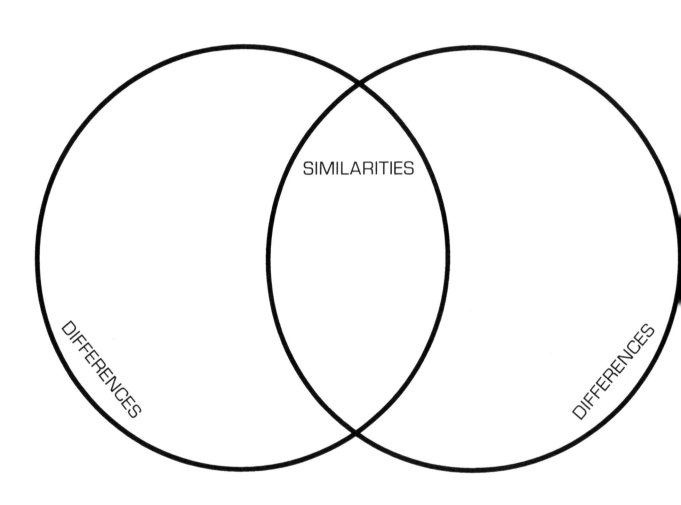

Name _____ Date _____

TIMELINE

DATE

EVENT
Draw lines to connect the event to the correct year on the timeline.

Name _____ Date

SEQUENCE OF EVENTS CHART

Event

Next Event

Next Event

Next Event

Next Event

Name _____ Date _____

Cause | Effect

•••••••►

•••••••►

•••••••►

Name _____ Date _____

ANSWER KEY

CHAPTER 1

BLACKLINE MASTER 1

1. the extent of the Mongol conquest in 1260

2. about 5000 miles

3. Kiev, Baghdad, Herat, Bukhara, Samarkand, Karakorum, and Beijing

4. Liegnitz, Mehir, Constantinople, Damascus, and Hangzhou

5. the Song

BLACKLINE MASTER 2

1. He promised that the wives and daughters of the bodyguards would be well cared for, and that they would have good horses and pastures. Horses and pastures were important to a good life for Mongols. They did not want or expect big houses or other expensive things.

2. Many, such as the people of Kiev, were killed.

3. He may have wanted to be sure that the guards focused on his needs, rather than the needs of their families. He may have been concerned for the families' welfare while he and his soldiers were away.

4. The people of Kiev probably fought against the Mongols rather than surrendering. The Mongols usually allowed those who surrendered without a fight to live.

5. The difference might be explained as Genghis Khan's loyalty to his own people.

CHAPTER TEST

A. 1. d **2.** b **3.** b **4.** a

B. 5. After the Mongols chose a target, they used their spy system to check out the strengths and weaknesses of their enemies.

6. The first fighting focused on control of the countryside and cities near the target.

7. If they couldn't break through their target's defenses, the Mongols pretended to flee. They then attacked the dispersed and unsuspecting armies.

C. Paragraphs will vary, but students' opinions should be supported with details from the text. Some students may suggest that the increase in trade did not in any way balance the loss of lives and the destruction of buildings, libraries, and records that wiped out knowledge of the past. Other students may feel that the increase in trade helped economies in Asia and Europe to grow, and therefore did balance the destruction.

CHAPTER 2

BLACKLINE MASTER 1

1. about 4500 miles

2. The Golden Horde should be circled.

3. The Yuan Dynasty should be underlined.

4. India, Burma, and Japan

5. the Black Sea

BLACKLINE MASTER 2

1. .The coffer is large and square and probably made out of gold. Inside is a huge, solid gold vase that holds many gallons. These items suggest that the court of Khubilai Khan held magnificent treasures.

2. They had to cover their mouths and noses with silk veils or cloths so that their breath could not harm his food and drink.

3. *Possible answer:* He wanted them to show respect, or he wanted them to be in a controlled position while he drank so that no one could sneak up and hurt him.

4. *Possible answer:* Marco Polo seems impressed, both by the apparent wealth of the Khan, and by his power. He describes the luxuries that surround the Khan, and he describes the ways in which the people around him are subservient to him.

CHAPTER TEST

A. 1. b **2.** d **3.** c **4.** c

B. 5. They wrote plays and operas and made paintings that subtly criticized the Mongols. For example, a painted image of bamboo symbolized the importance of bending but not breaking under the Mongols' harsh rule.

6. In 1368, the Ming forces overthrew the Yuan Dynasty and gained control of China.

C. Paragraphs will vary but should contain the following main ideas: Both men were brutal conquerors. Both came from severely difficult childhoods and probably learned to be tough early on. Both were very successful conquerors. However, Genghis Khan encouraged religious freedom and the pursuit of profitable trade. Timur, a Muslim, had very little religious tolerance and killed people with opposing views. He was excessively violent. Timur was proud of building up beautiful cities such as Samarkand and Bokhara, while Genghis Khan was generally anti-city.

CHAPTER 3

BLACKLINE MASTER 1

1. Their lands had decreased by 1582.

2. They controlled northern lands that had previously been held by the Teutonic Order.

3. Prague and Buda

4. about 200 miles

5. The Commonwealth bordered the Baltic and Black Seas, so they had some control of the sea trade in these regions.

6. *Possible answer:* Control of the Baltic Sea could lead to trade with the West.

BLACKLINE MASTER 2

1. Each Senator's army was ready to fight if an agreement could not be reached. The support of these armies was important because they would fight if there was not agreement about the new king.

2. *Possible answer:* Military forces would do battles to determine who the next king would be.

3. *Possible answer:* Everyone wanted to make sure that no one had more power than anyone else, and wanted to protect what they saw as rightfully theirs.

4. A public election would ensure that everyone who wanted to express a view could do so, and that everyone present could listen to the proceedings. It would also be clear that the king had been elected by all.

5. Most countries' monarchs were identified by heredity. Accept reasonable responses regarding which system is better, as long as students can support their answers with logical rules.

CHAPTER TEST

A. 1. c **2.** d **3.** a **4.** b **5.** c

B. 6. Poland was primarily Christian.

7. Lithuania followed a polytheistic religion that was seen as pagan by Christians.

8. Jadwiga was Christian and became convinced by Polish and Christian leaders to marry Jogaila, even though he was a pagan.

9. The marriage caused many Lithuanians, including Jogaila, to convert to Christianity.

CHAPTER 4

BLACKLINE MASTER 1

1. He praises St. Petersburg at the expense of Moscow. He indicates that St. Petersburg is young and powerful, while Moscow is older and past its prime.

2. He thought it would be "a heap of villages," but found it much larger and metropolitan.

3. They both praise St. Petersburg.

4. *Possible answer:* You could check whether the city had palaces in 1714, if it had sixty-odd thousand houses, and whether it was built in a short time.

5. *Possible answer:* Later governments may have wanted to return to a traditional capital; they may have recognized that St. Petersburg was more vulnerable to attack from the west.

BLACKLINE MASTER 2

1. He was handsome, tall, noble, quick-witted, a good conversationalist, friendly, and open.

2. She says that he is rustic, or coarse.

3. He wanted to modernize the Russian navy.

4. It means that he is witty in conversation.

5. Students' questions should deal with facts related to the letter.

6. *Possible answer:* Peter may have recognized that he could enjoy such interactions with women more often if the women were not separated from him.

CHAPTER TEST

A. 1. c 2. a 3. c 4. b 5. d

B. 6. Ivan may be described as "terrified" because he believed that he had many enemies. These fears led him to the terrible actions for which he is remembered.

7. Russia's location in the north gave it severe cold for much of the year. That made it unlikely that enemies would attack from the Arctic Sea, and so there was little need for a navy.

C. Essays will vary, but should mention the following similarities and differences: Both men were tsars of Russia, had absolute rule, punished enemies, fought to expand Russia, and killed their sons. Ivan the Terrible captured Kazan and Astrakhan, supported new architecture in Moscow, and established the *oprichniki*. Peter the Great traveled to Europe to learn ways of modernization, built St. Petersburg, supported Western education, allowed people with ability to rise in government, hired foreigners to form a stronger central government, and initiated reforms in society to benefit women

CHAPTER 5

BLACKLINE MASTER 1

1. Aurangzeb
2. The rivers provided water for drinking and bathing, and a means of transportation.
3. *Possible answer:* Controlling land on the coasts gave him access to trade routes.
4. Kabul
5. *Possible answer:* A traveler could travel northwest on the western tributary of the Ganges to reach Agra.

BLACKLINE MASTER 2

1. The speaker's husband left on a long trip to make money. He returned with only 1.5 copper coins, which he lost while swimming. After their family disowned them, the speaker tried to make a living with her spinning wheel. She was very successful and paid off all her husband's debts.
2. *Possible answer:* The other family members probably don't want to take on the poet's debts.
3. She started a business, spinning yarn or cloth.
4. The spinning wheel is important to the poet because it gave her a way to support her family.
5. Muslim women enjoyed many freedoms, including the right to run businesses and engage in commerce.

CHAPTER TEST

A. 1. c 2. d 3. a 4. c

B. 5. He taxed the land based on what it could produce. Therefore, it was a fair, graduated tax based on income. In flush years, farmers paid more than they did during drought years.

6. They were well educated, often more fully than their brothers and husbands.

C. Students may take either position in their essays, as long as they support it with valid reasons.

CHAPTER 6

BLACKLINE MASTER 1

1. the battles at Kosovo, Nicopolis, and Rumeli Hisari
2. the battles at Nicopolis and Rumeli Hisari
3. about 290 miles
4. The southern coastline was along the Mediterranean Sea. This provided access to trade.
5. It was by the Mediterranean Sea and on the sea route toward the Black Sea.

BLACKLINE MASTER 2

1. *Possible answer:* She gave thousands of gold pieces away.
2. The text says that she is pious, and she gave money in trust for Mecca and Medina.
3. Students' responses should be supported by information in the excerpts.
4. It means wise in handling practical matters, or having common sense.
5. She gave over the deeds of her seventy gardens and vineyards and her summer palaces and estates to her children and Melek's servants.

CHAPTER TEST

A. 1. c 2. d 3. a 4. c 5. d

B. 6. The Ottomans did not have a tradition of the oldest son inheriting the throne, so the son who got to the capital first and killed his brothers became the sultan.

7. The Christians felt that their children were being stolen from them, and the Ottomans believed they were giving these children great opportunities.

C. Essay should include the following information:
Beyazit "the Thunderbolt": fought in three of the most important battles in Ottoman history: at the Battle of Kosovo in 1387; at the Battle of Nicopolis in 1396; at the Battle of Ankara in 1402

Mehmet I: built grand new mosques

Mehmet II, "the Conqueror": captured Constantinople in 1453, defeating the Byzantines; rebuilt the city with new mosques, a palace, and other structures

CHAPTER 7

BLACKLINE MASTER 1

1. They were first frequented by scholars, poets, and people who had free time.
2. Over time, coffeehouses became places for all kinds of people to meet and pass time, from students and the unemployed to government officials and nobles.
3. The account seems to reflect the less formal regime that developed under Ahmet III, when appreciating life and relaxation were valued.
4. *Possible answer:* The description seems a lot like modern coffeehouses, where people go to meet, relax, enjoy their free time, and pursue their interests.

BLACKLINE MASTER 2

1. *Possible answer:* The author uses a respectful tone. He wants to show respect to his superior and gain approval for this budget.
2. The pilgrimage would be long and dangerous, and military personnel would be needed to protect the pilgrims on their journey.
3. It shows that these kinds of payments or bribes were accepted as part of the necessary funds needed on pilgrimages.
4. *Possible answer:* He probably wants to make it clear to his superior that he will keep track of and furnish records about how the funds were used.
5. *Possible answer:* By protecting the pilgrims, Ottoman rulers may have hoped to gain their loyalty.

CHAPTER TEST

A. 1. c 2. b 3. d 4. a

B. Ahmet III ruled during a time known as the Tulip Period, and his leadership was more relaxed and informal than earlier emperors. Unlike previous sultans, he welcomed European ideas. However, Janissaries and judges revolted, destroyed his palace, and weakened his rule.

C. *Possible answer:* While Suleyman was known as "the Law-Giver" by some, he is also called "the Magnificent" because of the way he built and established the Ottoman Empire. I think his support for building mosques, such as those by Sinan, and his support for the arts helped create a strong Ottoman presence that endured for centuries.

CHAPTER 8

BLACKLINE MASTER 1

1. *Possible answer:* The sorts of crimes being commited by the Portuguese in Brazil; the sorts of punishments inflicted on the Indians. Both could be checked in other records of the time.
2. Justice "will come from Heaven on all the inhabitants of Brazil" for the crimes against the American Indians.
3. *Possible answer:* The Portuguese had a negative effect on the lives of the American Indians.
4. *Possible answer:* The Portuguese punished the Indians as harshly as possible.
5. He felt that the Portuguese treated the Indians unfairly. Cardim lists the types of crimes that were "always" being committed against the Indians and specifies the "rigorous justice" against the Indians.
6. *Possible answer:* Cardim may have used the word "always" to emphasize the continuous nature of the misreatment and to prompt Portuguese officials to put an end to it.

BLACKLINE MASTER 2

1. He describes the sadness and sufferings of the captives. He explains that their sufferings increased "still more" when fathers were parted from sons, husbands from wives, and brothers from brothers.

2. *Possible answer:* Sadness, fear, despair, and sorrow. Some of them hung their heads, crying and looking only at one another. Others looked heavenward, crying out loudly, as if asking for help. Others hit their faces with their hands and threw themselves on the ground, while others expressed their grief by singing a sad song, as they would have in their own country.

3. Those in charge of separating the captives paid no attention to keeping friends and relations together. Thus, fathers were separated from sons, husbands from wives, and brothers from brothers.

4. *Possible answer:* Zurara probably thought they were heartless, inhumane, and disrespectful of others.

CHAPTER TEST

A. 1. c 2. b 3. d 4. a

B. 5. So the Portuguese set up "factories," trading centers with ports, warehouses, and administrators.

6. Portugal retained some places, but the Dutch East India Company took over the spice trade.

7. Portugal reestablished its independence.

C. Paragraphs will vary, but students' opinions should be supported with details from the text. Most students may agree with the author's point of view, pointing out that the monastery was built to celebrate Vasco da Gama's voyage to India, that wealth from the spice trade helped to finance its construction, and that some columns of the church are carved to look like the rope riggings on ships.

CHAPTER 9

BLACKLINE MASTER 1

1. New Granada (Columbia), Peru, and La Plata (Argentina)

2. the Spanish holdings in Europe and North Africa in 1550; its neighbors; major bodies of water

3. Manila, in the Philippines

4. *Possible answer:* The distances were vast, and transportation was slow.

5. northeast to Amsterdam and west across the English Channel

BLACKLINE MASTER 2

1. *Possible answer:* He is foolish; he has grand plans; he might be slightly insane.

2. *Possible answer:* Windmills were used to move millstones; the landscape included plains; people were religious.

3. that Don Quixote believes that he is going to fight giants, when they are actually windmills

4. *Possible answer:* It seems like they valued heroism and bravery, and they had a belief in God. By making Don Quixote crazed to battle a nonexistent enemy, the author may be criticizing the value placed on heroism and bravery in Spanish society.

CHAPTER TEST

A. 1. d 2. a 3. c 4. d

B. 5. The purpose of the Inquisition was to make sure newly converted Christians and other Catholics followed official Catholic doctrine.

6. The purpose of the missions was to convert Native Americans to Catholicism and European ways and, in return, have them work for the missions

C. 7. Epidemics broke out in Native American communities and many died.

8. Spain's prestige declined in Europe.

9. They rebelled and fought against the Spanish.

CHAPTER 10
BLACKLINE MASTER 1

1. Prague, Vienna, Buda, and Pest

2. They were about 175 miles apart.

3. the Balkan Mountains and the Danube River

4. They were all located on the Danube River.

5. These lands provided access to the Adriatic Sea.

BLACKLINE MASTER 2

1. He seemed to be more interested in taking revenge against the French king, rather than in helping the Habsburgs.

2. He did not think highly of the emperor and believed that Leopold was more interested in royal ceremonies than in the important issues of the day.

3. *Possible answer:* He may have enjoyed being a military leader. He may also have continued to be motivated by a desire to show the French that he would have been an effective military leader for them.

4. It reveals that he put considerable time and effort into planning military strategies, and that this planning helped make him a success.

CHAPTER TEST

A. 1. d 2. b 3. c 4. d 5. a

B. *Possible answer:* Kepler was an astronomer in the Habsburg Empire who determined that planets travel in elliptical paths around the sun. His Protestant beliefs caused him to be discriminated against in many ways. He eventually lost his position and was forced to leave his homeland.

CHAPTER 11
BLACKLINE MASTER 1

1. the Pamir Mountains and the Himalayas

2. They were most likely used for transportation, agriculture, and drinking water.

3. It was the capital of the Manchu Empire and close to the Yellow Sea.

4. They were along the coast or by major rivers.

5. *Possible answer:* Perhaps traders were going to different markets or wanted to take different paths through the mountains.

BLACKLINE MASTER 2

1. They believed that they were descended from the Yellow Emperor.

2. He feels that they are in an unfortunate position, living in poverty and distress and unable to help themselves.

3. He thinks that if they can work hard, some of them will become rich and honored.

4. He did not want the descendants to feel ashamed that one of their ancestors was a slave. You may wish to explain that Confucian tradition meant that these groups were excluded from the examination system, and therefore from higher office from generation to generation.

CHAPTER TEST

A. 1. c 2. d 3. d 4. c

B. 5. They tried to restore the belief in a female deity who comforted as a mother or grandmother might.

6. They developed a written language for the Manchu and schools where it was taught.

7. He sent a military campaign to Central Asia.

C. Students' essays should note that like most empires, the Manchu was unable to sustain its power due to changing rulers and outside influences. The Manchu Empire reached a peak, and then began to lose power and influence.

WRAP-UP TEST

1. Cause and effect charts should reflect the following points: under Genghis Khan, trade along the Silk Road was restored and rebuilt; cultures were again brought into contact with one another. The Mongols' success at making trade routes dependable allowed them to use paper currency rather than gold and silver.

2. Copernicus determined that the earth was not the center of the universe, but that planets circled the sun. Kepler later built upon the work of Copernicus and determined that planets traveled not in circles, but in elliptical paths in their orbits around the sun.

3. The physical geography of Poland and Lithuania did not include natural borders such as mountains and seas to protect them, so an alliance between them was beneficial to both. Reasons that their partnership was unlikely include very different religious beliefs and a history of fighting each other for control of Baltic trade.

4. Students should note that Alexis, Sophia, and Peter used Western ideas to reform or change nearly every aspect of Russian life, including education, the military, societal roles, government, and culture, and should include a clear description of one of these changes.

5. Paragraphs should discuss the fact that religious tolerance, especially under Akbar, allowed the empire to rule peoples of many different belief systems. Muslim art began to include human representations; education allowed Muslim women to be involved in politics, and Mughal art and architecture reflect many cultural influences.

6. Advantages should include the following: Janissaries received training as soldiers, and were respected as elite troops. As a strong, powerful unit, they had the influence to stage revolts against Ottoman rulers with whom they did not agree. Disadvantages should include the following: Janissaries were Christian boys taken from their families and forced to convert to Islam. They were forced to fight against Christians.

7. The Portuguese wanted to find a way to gain control of the spice trade, and so worked to sail around Africa to the east. Students may include descriptions of explorers such as Bartolomeo Dias, Gil Eanes, Vasco da Gama, or Afonso de Albuquerque.

8. Outlines should include the following details in support of the main idea: in 1492, Ferdinand and Isabella forced Muslims in Granada to convert or face expulsion. In the same year, all Jews who refused to convert to Christianity were expelled. As a result, many thousands of Muslims and Jews whose families had lived in the region for centuries left Spain.

9. Paragraphs on Poland and Lithuania may include examples such as the marriage of Jadwiga and Jogaila and the conversion of many Lithuanians to Christianity. Paragraphs on the Habsburg Empire may include examples such as royal marriages that resulted in lands linked by leaders with aligned religious beliefs and supported Catholic resistance to the Reformation.

10. Horses were key to transportation, the military, hunting, and were often important religious symbols. The Mongols were dependent on horses for nearly every aspect of life and became symbols of the empire's power; they were key to the Manchu in major hunts that trained leaders for battle; to the Lithuanians, horses were important religious symbols; in Spain, Isabella was known as "the Queen on horseback" because of her wide travels.

ANSWERS FOR THE STUDENT STUDY GUIDE
CHAPTER 1

Access
Main Idea: Genghis Khan was a hard man from a hard background.
>**Detail:** When he was a child, Tartars killed his father.
>**Detail:** Half-starved, he and his brother killed a stepbrother who took their food.
>**Detail:** He was captured by one clan and attacked by another.

Main Idea: Many factors made the Mongol army effective.
>**Detail:** The army used clever tactics and strict discipline.
>**Detail:** Mongol weapons were deadly, and a variety of arrows made the Mongols flexible fighters.
>**Detail:** The army was divided into squads for quick mobility.

Main Idea: An increase in trade balanced some of the destruction caused by the Mongols.
>**Detail:** The Mongols rebuilt Silk Road traffic, from Korea to Kiev.
>**Detail:** European merchants found their way back and forth in the China trade.
>**Detail:** The Mongols made the trade routes so dependable that paper money could be used.

Cast of Characters
Batu was Genghis Khan's grandson and the Mongol leader of Golden Horde controlling Russia.

Genghis Khan united the Central Asian clans and became their Khan, or leader. He led the Mongols in creating the largest land empire in history.

Khubilai Khan was the grandson of Genghis Khan. He unified China by 1279.

What Happened When?
1206: Temujin united the Central Asian clans and became the Khan, or leader, with the title of Genghis.

1220: Mongols capture Samarkand.

1227: Genghis Khan died.

1279: Khubilai Khan unified China.

Word Bank
1. maneuvers 2. ambush 3. campaign 4. conquered 5. coalition 6. invincibility

Word Play
brutality; Check students' sentences.

Critical Thinking
first box: 3 **second box:** 5 **third box:** 2 **fourth box:** 4 **fifth box:** 1

Identifying Figurative Language and Point of View
1. It turned fertile land into desolate land, some of which became a desert.
2. Juvaini would view the Mongols as destroyers of civilization because he describes negative effects of the Mongols' attack. For example, the destruction of the Iranian irrigation system turned a fertile area into desolate desert and caused most of the people in the area to die.
3. *Possible answer:* Juvaini says that a world that billowed with fertility was laid desolate "with one stroke," but it probably took some time before the fertile land turned into desert.
4. *Possible answer:* By emphasizing the destruction and devastation caused by the Mongols, Juvaini portrayed them as vicious and wasteful people.

All Over the Map
1. Be sure students have distinguished destructive actions from improvements, can explain the placement of icons on the map, have added dates correctly, have added a map legend, and have chosen a title that explains what the map shows.

CHAPTER 2

Access
Khubilai Khan:
Details about personality: powerful; liked to be in control
Details about accomplishments: controlled Yuan Dynasty; great wealth at his court; great power over his people
Timur:
Details about personality: hard and tough; good strategist; skilled fighter; intelligent; merciless; brutal; had a sense of humor
Details about accomplishments: conquered Aleppo, Damascus, Delhi, Baghdad, Isfhan, Sabzawaz; defeated the Golden Horde and the Ottomans

Cast of Characters
Marco Polo: Venetian merchant who traveled to China during Khubilai Khan's era
Timur (Tamberlane): violent 14th-century Central Asian conqueror; empire included parts of Iran, Iraq, Georgia, India, and Russia

Word Bank
1. administrators 2. allies 3. refugees 4. nomads 5. rivals 6. strategist

Word Play
deception, demise; Possible category: actions; Check students' sentences.

Critical Thinking
1. They were eager to conquer Korea.
2. Japan was never conquered by the Mongols.
3. After the fall of the Mongols, they created strong central governments that made their countries less vulnerable to conquest.
4. Ming forces eventually defeated the Yuan Dynasty in 1368, bringing the demise of the Mongol Empire.

Working with Primary Sources
1. He says that the invasion was caused by their sins.
2. There were no news reports, and the Mongols had no written language. Cities were spread apart across the steppes, so word traveled very slowly if at all.
3. *Possible answer:* Timur's advice shows that he understands that a show of force is not the only way to defeat an enemy. A smaller, strategically placed force can also lead to victory.

Identifying Point of View
4. The Kievan writer shows both fear and awe in his description of the Mongols. He seems to view their attack as a punishment from God.
5. *Possible answers:* He may have been planning a deceptive troop movement to fool an enemy. He may have been trying justify attacking with fewer troops than his generals believed were necessary.

All Over the Map
Check students' maps for accuracy. The area controlled by Timur should include Iran, Iraq, Georgia, Armenia, parts of India, and Russia.

CHAPTER 3

Access
Poland: primarily Christian; developed ties with Western Europe through royal marriages

Lithuania: followed pagan religion; many converted to Christianity

Similarities: were missed by the plague; lacked clear geographical borders; enemies were Tartars and Teutonic Knights; elected leaders through clan system; used royal marriages to unite lands

Cast of Characters
Jogaila: king of Poland and Lithuania, married to Jadwiga

Jadwiga: queen of Poland, ruled with Jogaila

Vytautas: Grand Duke of Lithuania

Nicolaus Copernicus: Polish astronomer

Jan Sobieski: king of Poland, saved Vienna from Turkish invasion

Word Bank
1. pagan 2. partition 3. modernizing 4. clan

Word Play
controversial, heretics; Check students' sentences.

Critical Thinking
5. the earth revolved around the sun
6. the earth was the center of the universe
7. of works forbidden to Catholics
8. *Possible answer:* It would be some time before most people accepted Copernicus's ideas.

Working with Primary Sources
1. The poet is addressing the magnates, because he describes how all "the wealth you amass" comes from "your serfs."
2. He thinks God has punished Poland for the harsh way that the serfs have been treated.
3. The magnates would have nothing at all without the efforts of their serfs.

All Over the Map
Check students' maps for accuracy.

CHAPTER 4

Access
1. They unified under the leadership of the city of Moscow.
2. Russia was able to begin its conquest of Siberia.
3. He formed the *oprichniki* to persecute his enemies.
4. He recruited foreign officers to train soldiers in new techniques.
5. They were persecuted and punished by Alexis, Sophia, and Peter.
6. They hired foreigners to teach accounting, record keeping, and foreign languages.
7. He put in place reforms to help Russian women.
8. He had them attend secular schools and sent nobles to European universities.
9. He moved the capital to St. Petersburg and built a city through hard labor.

Cast of Characters
Ivan the Terrible freed thousands of Russian prisoners from Kazan and Astrakhan.

Alexis recruited foreign soldiers to modernize the army.

Sophia sent 20,000 of the Old Believers into exile in Siberia.

Peter the Great founded St. Petersburg.

Word Bank
1. *terem* 2. *tsar* 3. *strelsty* 4. *boyars* 5. *oprichniki*

Word Play
Possible answer: The steppe is a large, flat treeless area of land found in southern Russia.

Critical Thinking
1. The facts listed describe cruel behaviors, so they support the generalization.
2. Rulers recruited foreigners to westernize Russia's military. The strelsty revolted.
3. *Possible generalization:* Often certain groups will resist efforts to change society.

Identifying Point of View
1. He feels that he's received evil and hatred in return for good and love.
2. He had a lot of tragedy in his life, beginning with his difficult childhood.
3. Ivan believed she had been poisoned, and he began to see enemies everywhere. He set up a secret police to persecute these enemies.
4. *Possible answer:* He seems to feel badly for himself, instead of for the people he killed and persecuted. I think he's only fooling himself so my view of him has not changed.

All Over the Map
Students should write five questions comparing two historical maps and answer their partners' questions correctly.

CHAPTER 5

Access
Possible details related to **Babur:**
   Detail: He was a fierce fighter, loyal and generous to his soldiers.
   Detail: He respected women, and relied on the advice of his mother and grandmother.
   Detail: He was innovative in his use of artillery.

Possible details related to **Akbar:**
   Detail: Through war and diplomacy, he expanded the empire greatly.
   Detail: He was Muslim, but he was extremely tolerant of other religions.
   Detail: He established a graduated land tax based on the productivity of the land.

Possible details related to **Aurangzeb:**
   Detail: He sought revenge against family members who opposed him.
   Detail: He reinstituted strict Muslim laws and taxed non-Muslims.
   Detail: He tore down Hindu temples and outlawed music and dancing.

Cast of Characters
Akbar: Mughal emperor who ruled 1556-1605, at height of empire

Aurangzeb: Last of the major Mughal rulers

Babur ("The Tiger"): Founder of the Mughal Empire

Word Bank
1. tyrant 2. sovereigns 3. artillery 4. pomp 5. diplomacy 6. rebellions

Word Play
sultanate; Check students' sentences for accuracy.

Critical Thinking
1. married a Hindu princess, practiced great tolerance with people of other religions, and tried to establish a new, inclusive religion.
2. he never learned to read
3. building her a magnificent tomb, the Taj Mahal.
4. the new emperor, Aurangzeb killed his unsuccessful brother and threw Shah Jahan into jail.
5. he had several Hindu temples torn down, outlawed music and dancing, and reinstituted the tax on non-Muslims.
6. of the magnificent art and architecture that was created during their era and survives today in India,
7. became writers and poets, advised government officials, and participated in business and trade.
8. their power diminished.

Working with Primary Sources
1. *Possible answer:* He thinks that meetings with learned men result in lively conversations and discussions. He thinks there is value in listening to a variety of opinions.
2. He thinks he needs to conquer enemies before they attempt to conquer him.
3. One quotation shows a lively intellect, interested in learning for its own sake. The other shows a warrior, intent on retaining his power.
4. Both show an analytical thought process, and a purposeful way of doing things.

All Over the Map
Check that icons for The Red Fort and the Jami Mosque are at Delhi, and the icon for the Taj Mahal is at Agra. Students' routes for a visit should include both locations and use correct directions to travel from one place to the other.

ANSWER KEY

CHAPTER 6

Access
Main Idea: The Ottoman Empire was full of contradictions.
> **Detail:** The homeland was on the steppes of Central Asia.
> **Detail:** The elite corps of the army and top government posts were former Christians from southern Europe.
> **Detail:** The sultans kept the women in a harem, but the Valide Sultan sometimes led the empire.

Main Idea: The Ottoman Turks ruled by the sword.
> **Detail:** Beyazit I fought in three of the most important battles in Ottoman history: at Kosovo, Nicopolis, and Ankara.
> **Detail:** After Beyazit's defeat at Ankara, Mehmet I fought his brothers to be the sultan and then killed them.
> **Detail:** The *devsirme* was held every seven years to round up and enslave Christian boys, who were trained for the Janissary or court positions.

Main Idea: The Ottoman Turks conquered and sacked Constantinople.
> **Detail:** The Ottomans used a cannon to weaken the Byzantines' defense.
> **Detail:** There were three days of looting and pillage after the city fell.
> **Detail:** Mehmet II conquered Constantinople and rebuilt it with Islamic architecture.

Cast of Characters
1. Beyazit, "the Thunderbolt": *Possible answer:* He was a sultan who could move his army quickly.
Mehmet II, "the Conqueror": *Possible answer:* He was a sultan who conquered Constantinople.
2. Timur and Beyazit fought for control of Ottoman lands at the Battle of Ankara. Beyazit was captured and died in prison.

Word Bank
1. *dhimmis* 2. *devsirme* 3. Valide Sultan 4. harem 5. Ulema

Word Play
6. *Possible answer:* Both are rulers, but a president is elected and a sultan seized control from his relatives.

Critical Thinking
Students' paragraphs should contrast Constantinople during the Byzantine era and the Ottoman era.

What Happened When?
1387 Battle at Kosovo
1396 Battle at Nicopolis
1402 Battle of Ankara
1453 defeat of Byzantium at Constantinople
1566–1666 "reign of women"

Identifying Point of View
1. He compares the army to a powerful river that floods, overwhelms the dikes, and causes infinite destruction.
2. *Possible answer:* They had a powerful army and had already conquered a lot of territory.
3. It expresses an opinion, because it is the author's belief, not a statement of fact.
4. *Possible answer:* You could read an encyclopedia article to see if the Austrian Empire fought with the Turkish army, or if the Turkish army was known for causing destruction during warfare.
5. His view might change if the Turks became less powerful.

In Your Own Words
Students' similes should help readers better understand or picture what the Ottoman Empire or the Turkish army was like.

All Over the Map
Check students' icons and dates for accuracy.

CHAPTER 7

Access
Check students' charts for thoughtful ideas and accuracy.

Cast of Characters
Suleyman: sultan of the Ottoman Empire during its Golden Age
Selim "the Grim": sultan and father to Suleyman, whom he tried to kill
Mimar Sinan: chief architect of the Ottoman Empire
Ahmet III: sultan of the Ottoman Empire during its Tulip Period

Word Bank
1. succession 2. campaign 3. siege 4. perimeter

Word Play
strait; Check students' sentences.

Critical Thinking
Possible answer: Suleyman is often referred to as the Law-Giver because he established a legal system and code of laws, the Kasun-i-Osman, which covered all areas of Ottoman life. In this way, Suleyman helped strengthen his growing empire.

Working with Primary Sources
1. She uses the comparison to show that she thinks that the many languages in Pera make it a confusing place to live.
2. *Possible answer:* She disapproves of the idea. By using the phrase, "and what is worse," she seems shocked by the idea that her own family knows so many of them.
3. It appears that she is not familiar with any beyond her own, since she describes what she hears as a "medley of sounds."
4. Her list of the many languages spoken in Pera illustrates how the Ottoman Empire came to include many lands, languages, and cultures.

All Over the Map
Check students' maps for accuracy. Be sure the following sites are noted correctly: battle where Suleyman's victory became known as "the tomb of the Hungarian nation." (Mohacs); the Mediterranean island where Suleyman's forces defeated Christian crusaders (Rhodes); the Mediterranean island that successfully fought off invasion by Suleyman's troops (Malta); the European city where General Mustafa's failed siege ended in disaster for the Ottomans (Vienna)

CHAPTER 8

Access
Event: 1415: Portuguese exploration down the African coast begins, sponsored by Henry the Navigator.
Event: 1484: Portuguese explorer Gil Eanes rounds Cape Bojador.
Event: 1488: Portuguese navigator and explorer Bartolomeu Dias rounds the southern tip of Africa, the Cape of Good Hope.
Event: 1498: Portuguese explorer Vasco da Gama commands the first European sea voyage to reach India in search of spices.
Event: 1500: Portuguese navigator Pedro Alvares Cabral takes over Brazil.
Event: 1510: Afonso de Albuquerque begins to establish a network of fortified cities for trade. The Indian city of Goa is the first of such cities.
Event: 1545: The Portuguese discover silver in Brazil, then gold and diamonds.

Cast of Characters
Check students' responses for accuracy.
Vasco Da Gama: Portuguese captain who reached India by sailing around Africa
Bartolomeu Dias: Portuguese captain who rounded southern tip of Africa
Henry "the Navigator": Portuguese prince who supported navigation and trade
Philip II: King of Spain who won the Portuguese throne after King Sebastian's death, sent Armada to attack England

Word Bank
1. crown 2. navigator 3. scurvy 4. treasuries 5. insurrections

Word Play
exploration; Check students' sentences.

Critical Thinking
1. d 2. c 3. g 4. a 5. e 6. b

Working with Primary Sources: Identifying Point of View
1. probably to Portuguese explorers, because the poem describes Portuguese exploration
2. *Possible answer:* possibly to show his respect for Prince Henry, the leader of Portuguese exploration
3. *Possible answer:* He probably felt proud, because Portugal was the trailblazer among other European nations in charting unexplored oceans and finding "new Isles and climates."

All Over the Map
Students should show the voyages led by the following Portuguese explorers and navigators: Gil Eanes, Bartolomeu Dias, Vasco de Gama, and Pedro Alvares Cabral. They should identify the fortified cities for trade that were established by Afonso de Albuquerque. Be sure students can explain the placement of routes on the map and correctly identify the explorers and navigators who made the voyages. Check that students added dates correctly, included a map legend, and chose a title that explains what the map shows.

CHAPTER 9

Access
Possible answers:
1. The Muslims lost their last stronghold in Spain.
2. Jews faced poor conditions whether they left or stayed as converses.
3. His voyages prompted other Spanish adventurers to explore the Americas.
4. The Church proposed the mission system to provide a better way of life.
5. Epidemics in the Americas killed many Native Americans.
6. They took part in a revolt.
7. Philip's agents managed to assassinate William.
8. The Spanish Armada was defeated.
9. The empire became weaker over time.

Cast of Characters
Isabella of Castile defeated the Muslims and took over Granada.

Ferdinand of Aragon married Isabella of Castile to strengthen the empire.

Charles V became the king of Spain and the Holy Roman Emperor.

Philip II sent the Spanish Armada to attack England.

Christopher Columbus got funding from Isabella to explore the western Atlantic.

Word Bank
1. Inquisition 2. *conversos* 3. trade winds 4. Iberian Peninsula 5. irrigation

Word Play
6. It comes from the Latin word *conquirere*, which means "to procure."

Critical Thinking
Students should create a chart in which they list facts, what they already know, and a conclusion about a group that was forcibly displaced by the Spanish.

Identifying Point of View
1. The missionary seems respectful, but frustrated.
2. Perhaps the missionary believes that Philip would have a better understanding of his empire if he made first-hand observations.
3. It is an opinion because it expresses the missionary's belief.
4. *Possible answer:* I know he was isolated and rarely traveled outside Spain. He relied on advisors for information.

All Over the Map
Check students' icons, arrows, and dates for accuracy.

CHAPTER 10

Access
1555: Peace of Augsburg allows rulers to determine the religion of their subjects
1618: Thirty Years' War begins; Habsburgs fight Protestant Germany and their allies over religious power
1620: Habsburgs defeat Czech forces at the Battle of White Mountain
1648: Thirty Years' War ends; the Treaty of Westphalia gives monarchs power to determine the religions of their lands
1683: Ottoman invasion of Vienna is defeated
1713: Charles VI issues the Pragmatic Sanction to allow Maria Theresa to be his successor
1740: Charles VI dies; Maria Theresa begins her rule

Cast of Characters
Johannes Kepler: Habsburg astronomer; discovered that planets moved in elliptical paths

Albrecht von Wallenstein: Habsburg general during the Thirty Years' War

Eugene of Savoy: Habsburg general who led army against Ottomans

Maria Theresa: Habsburg ruler; began military, tax, and education reforms

Word Bank
1. holdings 2. mercenary 3. traits 4. elliptical paths 5. assassins
6. discrimination

Critical Thinking
1. *Possible answer:* They accepted the Peace of Augsburg and fought the Thirty Years' War to maintain forms of religious control; under Maria Theresa, Jews and Protestants gained freedom from persecution.
2. *Possible answer:* With help from Polish forces, Vienna was saved from Ottoman invasion in 1683; led by Eugene of Savoy, the Habsburgs pushed back Ottoman forces from Central Europe.
3. *Possible answer:* Royal marriages did not always bring peaceful successions: Charles VI issued the Pragmatic Sanction in 1713 to allow his daughter, Maria Theresa, to lead the empire.

Drawing Conclusions
1. *Possible answer:* I think she was clearly aware that she had not gained experience as a ruler from her father, and that she faced great problems ahead.
2. *Possible answer:* She seems not at all sorry for herself, but, in fact, sounds very sensible and realistic. Her words do not sound as though she is looking for sympathy.
3. *Possible answer:* She sounds even more realistic, and very aware that the Prussians should be considered as enemies.
4. Accept answers that students can support. Some may choose her comments about the Prussians as an indication that she was cautious about trusting enemies.

All Over the Map
Check that students' maps reflect the following: the site of the Czech rebellion: Prague; the place that the Ottoman Empire tried to capture from the Habsburgs in 1683: Vienna; the name of the country that was freed from Ottoman rule, but then revolted under Habsburg rule: Hungary; the place that the Prussians invaded following the death of Charles VI: Silesia

CHAPTER 11

Access
Main Idea: The Manchus faced challenges when they took over the empire from the Ming Dynasty.

> **Detail:** The Ming left such problems as uncollected taxes, unread reports, and inept officials.

> **Detail:** The Manchus were outnumbered 2 million to 100 million.

> **Detail:** The Manchus wanted to keep their language and respect Chinese culture.

Main Idea: Manchu leaders tried to support their culture and keep it separate.

> **Detail:** They made Chinese men wear their hair in long pigtails.

> **Detail:** They developed a written Manchu language.

> **Detail:** They kept their clan system and marriage customs.

Main Idea: Kangxi and Qianlong led China in years of prosperity.

> **Detail:** Kangxi supported the Confucian idea that a ruler's duty was to bring welfare to the people.

> **Detail:** Qianlong tried to expand China's borders.

> **Detail:** During the first part of Qianlong's reign, the population was healthy, and trade brought wealth to the capital.

Cast of Characters
Students might say that **Qianlong** tried to model himself on his grandfather, Kangxi, in such ways as supporting scholarship.

Word Bank
Possible answers:
1. The Qing Dynasty understood how to use the Chinese administration.
2. The Manchu tried to change the custom of widow suicide by supporting a deity that was like a grandmother.
3. The Manchu rulers allowed people to worship at Buddhist temples, and they followed some Confucian beliefs.

Word Play
It comes from the Greek word *dynastēs*, which means "lord."

Critical Thinking
1. The author points out that both Shunzi and Kangxi were young and Manchu. The author points out the difference between Qianlong and Kangxi.
2. *Possible answer:* The technique helps readers to categorize the emperors' qualities, which makes them easier to remember.

Students' explanatory paragraphs should compare and contrast aspects of Manchu and Chinese culture, economics, or government. For instance, they could note that both Manchu and Chinese dynasties were run by a central leader, or they could contrast the Manchu's less-rigid and the Chinese more-rigid class systems

Identifying Point of View
1. how to maintain peace in the empire
2. He might have valued civilian officers who were not greedy and military officers who were brave.
3. He was part of a minority culture and had to protect the empire from enemies within and without.
4. *Possible answer:* Perhaps he believed that he would have more control over the ethnic Chinese majority if they saw ethnic Chinese as military leaders.

In Your Own Words
Students' journal entries should reflect the understanding that Kangxi traveled the provinces to bring welfare to the people. He also wanted to maintain Manchu control over the Chinese majority.

All Over the Map
Check students' questions based on the map scale and trade routes for accuracy.

Made in the USA
San Bernardino, CA
05 September 2013